SPOTTISWOODE: LIFE AND LABOUR ON A BERWICKSHIRE ESTATE, 1753–1793

This book has been sponsored by Tom Farmer CBE, Kwik-Fit Holdings plc, in recognition of all the support and good work carried out by Tom Barry for the benefit of the community in Scotland.

SPOTTISWOODE:

Life and Labour on a Berwickshire Estate, 1753–1793

Introduction by Douglas Hall
Commentary by Tom Barry

TUCKWELL PRESS

First published in 1997 in Great Britain by
Tuckwell Press Ltd,
The Mill House, Phantassie,
East Linton, East Lothian EH40 3DG,
Scotland

ISBN 1 898410 96 8
British Library Cataloguing-in-Publication Data
A catalogue record for this book is available
on request from the British Library

Typeset by Carnegie Publishing, 18 Maynard St, Preston
Printed and bound by
Cromwell Press, Broughton Gifford, Melksham, Wiltshire

Contents

Preface

THE JOURNAL, diary or ledger which forms the basis of this book was offered to me in 1978 by a gentleman now dead. It came from the papers of the Spottiswoode family of Spottiswoode, Berwickshire, which were dispersed in 1935. Many are now in the National Library of Scotland, but others besides this volume no doubt disappeared, and many were burned.

The diary is made from hand-made rag paper, much of it watermarked *Honi soit qui mal y pense*, and approximates to modern foolscap size, with plain board covers. The ink has not faded except where an old quill has apparently failed to hold the ink or the ink mixture has been too thin. The entries cover the period from 1753 to 1793, which means that it was kept during the lairdship of John Spottiswoode of that Ilk, the second in the line of four lairds of that name who possessed the estate from 1700 to 1866. From the frequent use of the first person singular, it appears that most of the entries were written by the Laird himself, and thus that he was concerning himself with the most minute details of running the estate. Where other hands can be made out, the writers are more likely to be members of his family than employees.

It was considered by many south of the Border that Scottish agriculture around 1750 was a hundred years behind England's. Consequently there were few compliments from travellers such as Dr Johnson who toured Scotland with James Boswell in 1773, or Thomas Pennant who did so in 1769. The importance of this diary/journal is much enhanced because it was compiled during the great days of the Agricultural Improvers. John

Spottiswoode is not included in the accepted list of these, but it could be argued that he merits inclusion. It is not too far-fetched to suggest that he picked up his knowledge as he went along because there were several Improvers in the Merse and East Lothian at that time, who lived not too far away, such as the Earl of Haddington, Lord Kames and John Cockburn of Ormiston. There were others, in England, from whom John could have gained knowledge by correspondence. In those days of poor communications and general ignorance, a man could learn much from what he saw if, for example, he were to make a ten-day journey to London by coach. John Spottiswoode had his own coach and did make journeys to London in it.

The diary contains a variety of loose notes. Among these is a most interesting record of the Spottiswoode grain yield. Not only is this an early example of yield but it shows a most satisfactory result. At the top of the paper, it is noted that all quantities are in 'Teviotdale measure'. This is to avoid confusion as there were several measures in use at the time, such as Linlithgow, Duns, Kelso, Glasgow, Lanark and Haddington as well as Teviotdale. In England there were several measures as well, but Winchester was the most used. Also noted on loose sheets were a statement of a debt owing to Mrs Roberton (presumably John's daughter Rachael); a statement of purchases of lime, a record of port wine consumption and various calculations which were later transferred to the diary.

At a point in my work on the commentary I met with Douglas and Matilda Hall who lived at Spottiswoode for twenty years, and who were already researching the history of the estate and the family. Douglas Hall has brought together the results of his work and some of mine in the section of this book named *The House of Spottiswoode*.

Tom Barry

Acknowledgements

T HE AUTHORS wish to acknowledge the help of the following in the preparation and publication of this book:

His Grace the Duke of Buccleuch and Queensberry, KT, whose antecedent, Lord John Scott, married Alicia Anne Spottiswoode (the 'wise woman of Spottiswoode' of this book), has very kindly allowed us to launch the book at Bowhill.

Mr Tom Farmer CBE has most generously supported the costs of publication.

Mr John Herbert Spottiswoode, Lady John Scott's great-nephew, has been in touch with both authors over several years. He is the source of many of the illustrations and has relayed numerous traditions and stories of the house of Spottiswoode handed down from previous generations, not all of which have been incorporated in the book.

Mrs Dorothy Spottiswoode Doré, Secretary of the Spottiswoode Family History Society, has provided the family trees and has striven to keep this account on the genealogical rails. She cannot be held responsible for any derailments that may be discovered in the Introduction.

Marianna Spottiswoode Lines, artist and historian, and author of a one-woman play on Lady John Scott, discovered the portrait of John Spottiswoode II, now attributed by James Holloway to William Denune of Dumfries, and reproduced here for the first time.

Christopher Ruffle, present owner of Archbishop Spottiswoode's castle at Dairsie, willingly gave access to it before and after its rebuilding.

Mr and Mrs Logan McDougal of Blythe and the residents of Spottiswoode have tolerated our curiosity and helped keep the traditions of the place alive.

Among others who have helped or advised on the antiquarian and architectural aspects of the subject are: W A Brogden, Hugh Cheape of the Royal Museum of Scotland, Kitty Cruft, J E Ingram of the Colonial Williamsburg Foundation, James Macaulay, Douglas Sandford of Mary Washington College, Fredericksburg, and staff of the National Library of Scotland and the Royal Commission on the Ancient and Historical Monuments of Scotland.

Tom Barry wishes to acknowledge the help he has had from the National Farmers' Union of Scotland, Arthur Anderson of BBC Aberdeen, Michael Cox, the late Ian Grant, Fordyce Maxwell, Gerry and Monica Minchella, Mrs S L Mowat and Geoff and Holly Quick.

Finally, our most grateful thanks are reserved for Maureen Barry and Matilda Hall (Matilda Mitchell) for endless support. Matilda was one of the first to begin to explore the documentary sources for the story of Spottiswoode.

Illustrations

Tree (MASTER)

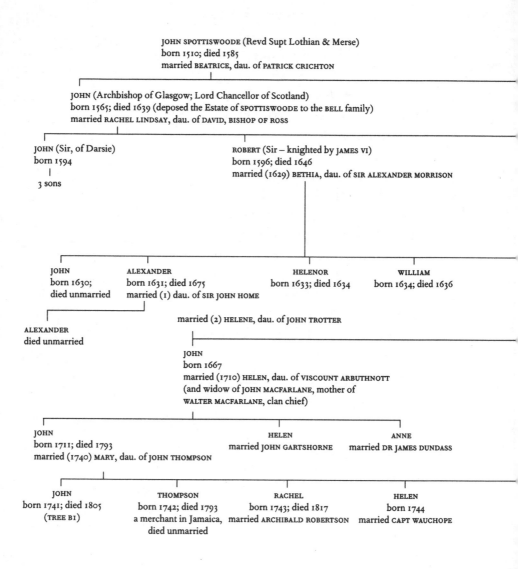

JOHN SPOTTISWOODE (Revd Supt Lothian & Merse)
born 1510; died 1585
married BEATRICE, dau. of PATRICK CRICHTON

JOHN (Archbishop of Glasgow; Lord Chancellor of Scotland)
born 1565; died 1639 (deposed the Estate of SPOTTISWOODE to the BELL family)
married RACHEL LINDSAY, dau. of DAVID, BISHOP OF ROSS

JOHN (Sir, of Darsie)
born 1594

3 sons

ROBERT (Sir – knighted by JAMES VI)
born 1596; died 1646
married (1629) BETHIA, dau. of SIR ALEXANDER MORRISON

JOHN
born 1630;
died unmarried

ALEXANDER
born 1631; died 1675
married (1) dau. of SIR JOHN HOME

HELENOR
born 1633; died 1634

WILLIAM
born 1634; died 1636

ALEXANDER
died unmarried

married (2) HELENE, dau. of JOHN TROTTER

JOHN
born 1667
married (1710) HELEN, dau. of VISCOUNT ARBUTHNOTT
(and widow of JOHN MACFARLANE, mother of
WALTER MACFARLANE, clan chief)

JOHN
born 1711; died 1793
married (1740) MARY, dau. of JOHN THOMPSON

HELEN
married JOHN GARTSHORNE

ANNE
married DR JAMES DUNDASS

JOHN
born 1741; died 1805
(TREE B1)

THOMPSON
born 1742; died 1793
a merchant in Jamaica,
died unmarried

RACHEL
born 1743; died 1817
married ARCHIBALD ROBERTSON

HELEN
born 1744
married CAPT WAUCHOPE

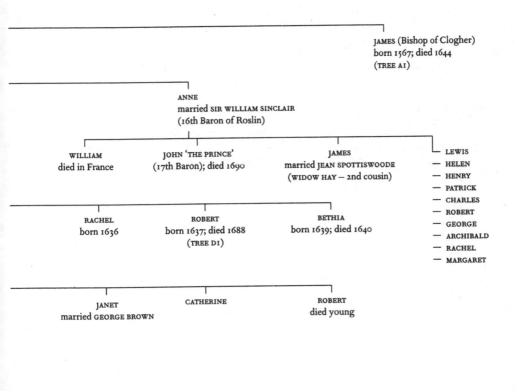

JAMES (Bishop of Clogher)
born 1567; died 1644
(TREE AI)

ANNE
married SIR WILLIAM SINCLAIR
(16th Baron of Roslin)

WILLIAM
died in France

JOHN 'THE PRINCE'
(17th Baron); died 1690

JAMES
married JEAN SPOTTISWOODE
(WIDOW HAY – 2nd cousin)

— LEWIS
— HELEN
— HENRY
— PATRICK
— CHARLES
— ROBERT
— GEORGE
— ARCHIBALD
— RACHEL
— MARGARET

RACHEL
born 1636

ROBERT
born 1637; died 1688
(TREE DI)

BETHIA
born 1639; died 1640

JANET
married GEORGE BROWN

CATHERINE

ROBERT
died young

MARGARET
born 1747
married JAMES EYRE

MACFARLANE
born 1748
married WILLIAM LAWSON

ANNE
born 1749; died 1793

ROBERT
born 1752; died 1816
(TREE CI)

Tree A1

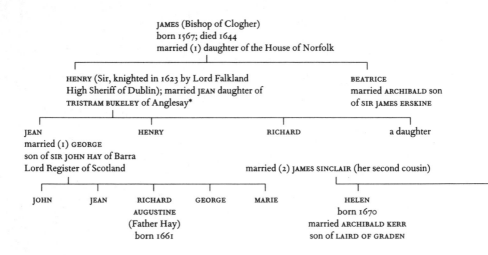

JAMES (Bishop of Clogher)
born 1567; died 1644
married (1) daughter of the House of Norfolk

HENRY (Sir, knighted in 1623 by Lord Falkland
High Sheriff of Dublin); married JEAN daughter of
TRISTRAM BUKELEY of Anglesay*

BEATRICE
married ARCHIBALD son
of SIR JAMES ERSKINE

JEAN
married (1) GEORGE
son of SIR JOHN HAY of Barra
Lord Register of Scotland

HENRY

RICHARD

a daughter

married (2) JAMES SINCLAIR (her second cousin)

JOHN   JEAN   RICHARD   GEORGE   MARIE
                AUGUSTINE
                (Father Hay)
                born 1661

HELEN
born 1670
married ARCHIBALD KERR
son of LAIRD OF GRADEN

---

*Pedigree through the BUKELEYS to JOHN OF GAUNT (4th son of EDWARD III) married (2) ELIZABETH STAUNTON (widow PERKINS)

JAMES

ELIZABETH
married (1) JAMES HEIRONE
married (2) THOMAS GOLBORNE

MARY
married COLONEL ABRAHAM CRICHTON

JAMES
(Page of Honour to QUEEN MARIE)
born c 1671; died Battle of
Boyne 1690

ALEXANDER
born 1672
(Laird of Roslin)
married JEAN SEMPILL

ANN
died young

THOMAS
BORN 1675

Tree B1

JOHN (Solicitor of Sackville St, London)
born 1741; died 1805
married MARGARET PENELOPE 10 Jun 1779 dau. of WILLIAM STRAHAN

JOHN	MARGARET JANE	WILLIAM	GEORGE	MARY
born 1780; died 1866	born/died 1781	born 1782	born 1784; died 1857	born 1785
married HELEN 1809		died 1800	(Lt. Col. British Army)	
dau. of ANDREW WAUCHOPE				

ALICIA ANNE	JOHN	ANDREW	MARGARET PENELOPE
born 1810; died 1900	born 1811	born 1812; died 1862	born 1813; died 1839
married 1836 LORD JOHN	(Officer	(Capt. 9th Lancers	married 1834 SIR HUGH HUME
DOUGLAS MONTAGUE SCOTT,	Grenadier Guards)	Col. 1st Dragoon Guards) CAMPBELL	
son of Duke of Buccleuch		married 1845 Cawnpore	(5th Bart-Marchmont)
		EMILY JANE CAMPBELL	

JOHN WILLIAM
born Sept 1848
Warwick

HELEN
born April 1847 Cawnpore
died Nov. 1882
married 1873
CAPT. CHARLES
JAMES HERBERT
(late Grenadier
Guards)

HELEN HUME CAMPBELL
born 1835; died 1875
married 1854
SIR GEORGE
WARRENDER
(6th Bart)

JOHN	GEORGE JOHN	HUGH VALDAVE	JULIAN	ALICE	ELEANOR
born 1859	SCOTT	born 1868	MARGARET	HELEN	CHARLOTTE
died 1894	born 1860		MAITLAND		
	married 1894				

HELEN JANE HERBERT
born 1879
died young

JOHN RODERICK
CHARLES HERBERT
(Lt. R.N.V.R.)
born Oct. 1882; died Jan. 1946
married (1) 1906 EVELINE ANNE VENABLES-KYRKE (divorced)
married (2) 1915 HYLDA MARJORIE VENABLES-KYRKE (died 1931)
married (3) 1933 HYLDA FLORENCE TWIST

RONALD ANDREW
born 1899
married 1923
IRIS FARNELL
WATSON

JOHN TERRENCE
KENNEDY HERBERT
SPOTTISWOODE
born 1917

SUSAN DIERDRE
ANDREA HERBERT
SPOTTISWOODE
born 1943

HUGH IAN
born 1924

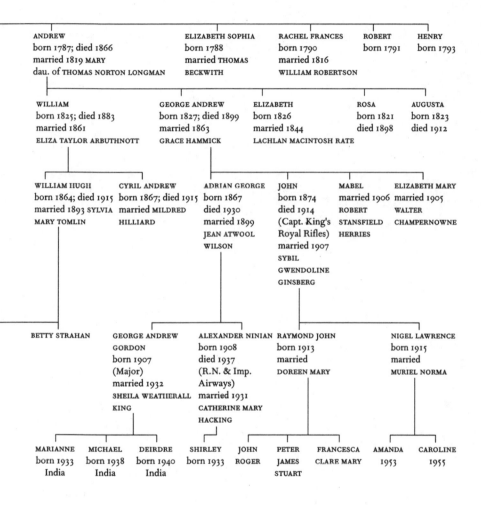

ANDREW
born 1787; died 1866
married 1819 MARY
dau. of THOMAS NORTON LONGMAN

ELIZABETH SOPHIA
born 1788
married THOMAS
BECKWITH

RACHEL FRANCES
born 1790
married 1816
WILLIAM ROBERTSON

ROBERT
born 1791

HENRY
born 1793

WILLIAM
born 1825; died 1883
married 1861
ELIZA TAYLOR ARBUTHNOTT

GEORGE ANDREW
born 1827; died 1899
married 1863
GRACE HAMMICK

ELIZABETH
born 1826
married 1844
LACHLAN MACINTOSH RATE

ROSA
born 1821
died 1898

AUGUSTA
born 1823
died 1912

WILLIAM HUGH
born 1864; died 1915
married 1893 SYLVIA
MARY TOMLIN

CYRIL ANDREW
born 1867; died 1915
married MILDRED
HILLIARD

ADRIAN GEORGE
born 1867
died 1930
married 1899
JEAN ATWOOL
WILSON

JOHN
born 1874
died 1914
(Capt. King's
Royal Rifles)
married 1907
SYBIL
GWENDOLINE
GINSBERG

MABEL
married 1906
ROBERT
STANSFIELD
HERRIES

ELIZABETH MARY
married 1905
WALTER
CHAMPERNOWNE

BETTY STRAHAN

GEORGE ANDREW
GORDON
born 1907
(Major)
married 1932
SHEILA WEATHERALL
KING

ALEXANDER NINIAN
born 1908
died 1937
(R.N. & Imp.
Airways)
married 1931
CATHERINE MARY
HACKING

RAYMOND JOHN
born 1913
married
DOREEN MARY

NIGEL LAWRENCE
born 1915
married
MURIEL NORMA

MARIANNE
born 1933
India

MICHAEL
born 1938
India

DEIRDRE
born 1940
India

SHIRLEY
born 1933

JOHN
ROGER

PETER
JAMES
STUART

FRANCESCA
CLARE MARY

AMANDA
1953

CAROLINE
1955

© 1997 DOROTHY SPOTTISWOODE DORE

Tree C1

ROBERT (London Solicitor)
born 1752; died 1816
married 1777 CECILIA MOSSMAN of Auctyfardel, Co. Lanarks.

JOHN
(London Solicitor 1802–1825)

HUGH (H.E.I.C.S.)
born 1782; died at sea on passage to Cape, April 1820
married Feb 1805 Calcutta
HARRIETT dau. of BURTON SMITH

CECILIA
married ROBERT
WORSLEY

ELIZABETH HELEN
born Nov. 1805
Calcutta
married 1824
SIR RICHARD JENKINS
G.C.B.

CECILIA
born 1807
Calcutta
married 1824
SIR MAURICE STACK
MAJ. GEN.

ARTHUR COLE
born 1808 Ganjam India
died 1874 Hastings
(Maj. Gen. Bengal Army)
married Aug. 1834 Bengal
JESSEY ELIZA dau. of
LT. GEN. LAMBERT LOVEDAY

HENRY
born 1809
Madras
died 24/25 May 1857
(Lt. Col. Bengal Army)
(died during the Indian
Mutiny)

HELEN CECILIA
born 1836
India

ARTHUR LAMBERT
born 1838
India

ROBERT COLLINSON
born 1841
India
died 1936
(Col. 10th
Hussars)
married 1887
ELIZA
TURNBULL

CATHERINE AUGUSTA
born 1845
India
died 1848
India

LAMBERT LOVEDAY
born 1846
India
died 1871
India
(Lt. 107th
Regt)

ANNE LOUISA
born 1847
India
died 1867
Scotland

HENRY PHILLIPSON
born 1849
India
died 1917
England
married 1891
BEATRICE
PROWER
(born 1860
died 1955)

CONSTANCE
born 1848
India
died 1848
India

ARTHUR
born 1892; died 1940
(Solicitor.
M.C. & Bar)

JOHN
born 1896
(Brigadier. M.C.)
married 1925
JOAN GRYLLS

MARGARET
born 1894
married 1921
CAPT. JOHN COGSWELL
BOARDMAN R.N.

HUGH
born 1904
died 1961
(Nigerian Civil Service)
married 1935 HILDEGARD
ENID MORRISON of Capetown

ROBERT ANTHONY
born 1926

DAVID MERVYN
born 1928

CHARLES
born 1932

JOHN NINIAN
born 1936
died 1959

BRIAN HUGH
born 1939

CHRISTOPHER MERVYN
born 1941

STEPHEN MORRISON
born 1947

HELEN

MARIA
died March 1834

EMILY BARCLAY
born India
married 1830
DR. ROBERT PINKEY
(I. Med Service)

MOLYNEUX CAPEL
(Lt. Col. Bengal Army)
born 1816 India
died 1890 Southsea
married CHARLOTTE
MARIA SINCLAIR

HUGH
born 1818 Macao, China
Capt. Bengal Army
died 28 May 1857
(died during Indian Mutiny)

MARY
CONGREVE
born 1850
India
died 1853

CECILIA
MAIMEE
born 1852
India
married
DOCTOR
HUMPHREYS

WILLIAM
DONALD
born 1859

ARTHUR
DONALD
born 1859
Twins
died
1860
Kandy
Ceylon

HUGHSTALK
born 1852
Sangor
India

CECILIA
born India
married
MAJOR
GROVES

SARAH
MARIA
born India

ARTHUR
ANDREW
born India
died 1919
(Colonel
Bengal
Army)

CHARLES
JOHN
(Maj. Bengal
Army)
born India
died Cork
Ireland
Married
CLEMENTIN
JANE SIMS

MOLYNEUX
CAPEL
born India
died 1875
Madras
(Lt. 43rd
Regt.
Bengal
Army)

LT JOHN MOLYNEUX
SPOTTISWOODE GROVES
born India 1870
died 1894
Bangalore
(XVIII Hussars)

ARTHUR ULRIC
MOLYNEUX CAPEL
born 1896
died 1935
(Maj. 2/5 Gurkha
Rifles)

CYNTHIA
MARIA
born 1903
died Ascot
1953

Tree D1

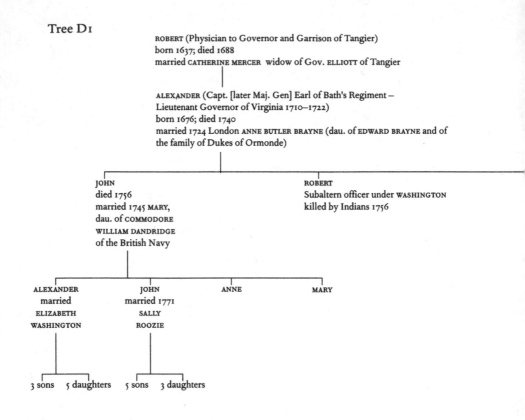

ROBERT (Physician to Governor and Garrison of Tangier)
born 1637; died 1688
married CATHERINE MERCER widow of Gov. ELLIOTT of Tangier

ALEXANDER (Capt. [later Maj. Gen] Earl of Bath's Regiment –
Lieutenant Governor of Virginia 1710–1722)
born 1676; died 1740
married 1724 London ANNE BUTLER BRAYNE (dau. of EDWARD BRAYNE and of
the family of Dukes of Ormonde)

JOHN
died 1756
married 1745 MARY,
dau. of COMMODORE
WILLIAM DANDRIDGE
of the British Navy

ROBERT
Subaltern officer under WASHINGTON
killed by Indians 1756

ALEXANDER
married
ELIZABETH
WASHINGTON

JOHN
married 1771
SALLY
ROOZIE

ANNE

MARY

3 sons 5 daughters 5 sons 3 daughters

ANNE CATHERINE
born 1726
married 1745 BERNARD MOORE
from whom is descended Confederate
General ROBERT E. LEE

DOROTHEA
married 1747 CAPT. NATHANIEL WEST
DANDRIDGE of the British Army

4 sons   4 daughters

5 sons   6 daughters

Heir of Entail
on
(TREE B.1)

Activated on the death of JOHN SPOTTISWOODE of

Sons of JOHN SPOTTISWOODE and MARGARET PENELOPE STRAHAN

JOHN
born 1780; died 1866
married HELEN WAUCHOPE 13th Sept. 1809 (1)

ALICIA ANNE (2)
born 1810 London; died 1900 Spottiswoode
married 16 March 1836 to LORD JOHN MONTAGUE SCOTT,
died 1860 son of DUKE OF BUCCLEUCH; d.s.p.

JOHN
born 1811
(Officer Grenadier Guards); d.s.p.

HELEN JANE (3)
born 19 April 1847 Cawnpore, India
died November 1882
married 30 Dec. 1873 St. James, Westminster
CAPT CHARLES JAMES HERBERT widower late of
Grenadier Guards (died 1891)
son of HENRY ARTHUR HERBERT M.P.

HELEN JANE HERBERT
born c.1878; died young

Heir of Entail
1. wife HELEN
2. daughter ALICIA ANNE
3. granddaughter HELEN JANE
4. granddaughter HELEN HUME
5. brother ANDREW (Heir male SPOTTISWOODE descent)

JOHN RODDERICK CHARLES HERBERT became his mother's
Heir of Entail and added SPOTTISWOODE to his name in June 1900

Present heir male SPOTTISWOODE, HUGH IAN SPOTTISWOODE born 1924

Sackville Street, London and of Spottiswoode, Berwickshire

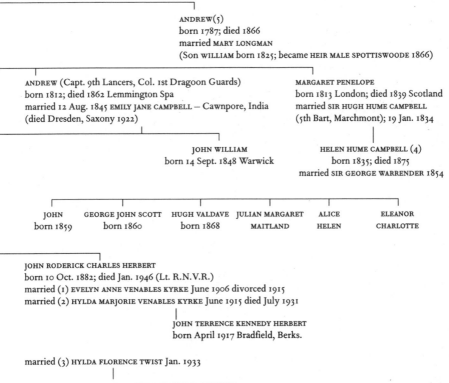

ANDREW(5)
born 1787; died 1866
married MARY LONGMAN
(Son WILLIAM born 1825; became HEIR MALE SPOTTISWOODE 1866)

ANDREW (Capt. 9th Lancers, Col. 1st Dragoon Guards)
born 1812; died 1862 Lemmington Spa
married 12 Aug. 1845 EMILY JANE CAMPBELL — Cawnpore, India
(died Dresden, Saxony 1922)

MARGARET PENELOPE
born 1813 London; died 1839 Scotland
married SIR HUGH HUME CAMPBELL
(5th Bart, Marchmont); 19 Jan. 1834

JOHN WILLIAM
born 14 Sept. 1848 Warwick

HELEN HUME CAMPBELL (4)
born 1835; died 1875
married SIR GEORGE WARRENDER 1854

| JOHN | GEORGE JOHN SCOTT | HUGH VALDAVE | JULIAN MARGARET | ALICE | ELEANOR |
| born 1859 | born 1860 | born 1868 | MAITLAND | HELEN | CHARLOTTE |

JOHN RODERICK CHARLES HERBERT
born 10 Oct. 1882; died Jan. 1946 (Lt. R.N.V.R.)
married (1) EVELYN ANNE VENABLES KYRKE June 1906 divorced 1915
married (2) HYLDA MARJORIE VENABLES KYRKE June 1915 died July 1931

JOHN TERRENCE KENNEDY HERBERT
born April 1917 Bradfield, Berks.

married (3) HYLDA FLORENCE TWIST Jan. 1933

SUSAN DEIRDRE ANDREA HERBERT
born August 1943

PART ONE

The House of Spottiswoode

I

The Lammermuir Lairds

THE HOUSE of Spottiswoode stood on the southern edge of Lammermuir from 'time out of mind', looking over the folds of land falling
away to the Merse, a view terminated on clear days by the line of the
Cheviots in England. The Royal Burgh of Lauder, now a small town on
the busy A68, is five miles to the west, the village of Gordon about the
same distance to the south on the road to Kelso. Although secluded,
backed by the roadless expanse of the Lammermuirs, the place is not
inaccessible, since it is bounded by the road from Edinburgh to Coldstream, now the A697 and still the most direct route from the Scottish
capital to the English border. In Scotland's first age of improvement the
Spottiswoode lairds were interested in road-building; there is a tradition
that one went into partnership with Macadam, but this may be a confusion
with another member of the family. It was not coincidence that the present
roads from Duns and Kelso converge on the Coldstream turnpike on
Spottiswoode land, for they were both surveyed in the late eighteenth century. Both would have paid tolls to the estate. Road-building fever went
on for some decades more. In the Spottiswoode papers now in the National
Library of Scotland there is a map of a 'proposed new line of road between
Soutra Mains farm house and Spottiswoode Gate' dated 1829 (NLS MS
2952).

In the annals of Spottiswoode this is the day before yesterday. Before
looking at their origins, it may be practical to consider the spelling of the
name. There are many variants, Spottiswoode, Spottiswood, Spotiswode
and others. The variations have little significance, and cannot be used as

a guide to the different branches of the family. For all the possible spellings, there was only one pronunciation: Spotswood. This was the form sensibly adopted by members of the family who went overseas, where the old Scots plural or genitive *is* (birdis, kingis etc), with its silent *i*, was not likely to be recognised. In the nineteenth century when uniformity of spelling became the rule, both the Scottish and English branches seem to have settled down to the spelling Spottiswoode, to which the final *e* gave an antiquarian flavour. This is the spelling used in this book, except in reference to Governor Spotswood of Virginia, or in quoting directly from a source. Modern usage sometimes prefers Spottiswood in reference to the place, rather than the family.

'The fact that St Ninian came from Spottiswood . . .' begins the account of the family in *Burke's Landed Gentry*. Few families seem to have been more proud of their antiquity, but there is no evidence to support this claim to the saint, except the frequent occurrence of the name Ninian in the history of the family. Since the sixteenth century, however, the name John predominates over all others, and was almost always given to the eldest son. From 1700 to 1866 the estate lay in the possession of four successive lairds of that name. That was the golden age of Spottiswoode. Yet in 1700 there had already been Spottiswoodes at Spottiswoode for over 400 years.

Anciently, Berwickshire, with the Merse, was part of Northumbria. Later it was the part of Scotland most open to the introduction of feudalism through the distribution of land by the Norman kings. It is supposed the first Spottiswoodes of that Ilk got their land in that way. The plain modern village of Gordon recalls the existence in those parts of the powerful family of that name, before they established their power base in the north. The Spottiswoodes may have been their vassals, for both families carry a boar's head on their arms; later, at least part of the estate lay in the feudal dominion of the Maitlands of Thirlestane.

These events are, in an exact sense, 'out of mind', and the efforts of the proud antiquarian lairds of the golden age, with their charters and deeds around them, failed to establish an exact line of succession. The written history seems to have begun in 1296 when a Robert de

Spottiswoode affixed his seal (representing a whole boar, not merely a boar's head) to the so-called Ragman's Roll, that is, as a landowner with followers, in common with most of his peers, he swore fealty to the English King Edward I, who had beaten the Scots into submission over a period of five years. His family must have been in place for several generations already, at a time when there was little written record kept in Scotland. After him, the name occurs in rolls and charters, but not with any clear picture of succession to the estate or headship of the family. The history of any family in dangerous and lawless times must have been far more complex and often seamier than the neat tables and trees of family piety and Victorian genealogy would suggest. Indeed at all times there are skeletons in the cupboard, more children than can be accounted for in Burke, for example. In the earliest part of their history the Spottiswoodes seem to have had the characteristics of a clan rather than a modern landed family, though never of course a clan in the strict sense of the word as applied to Highland families.

As written records become more common, they tend to support the picture that imagination, and acquaintance with the place, serve to build up. The Borders, even the somewhat safer eastern marches, were certainly as dangerous in the sixteenth century as in the fourteenth, perhaps more so. Later references to Spottiswoode sometimes locate it in the Merse, a miry but settled plain, as productive as primitive agriculture would allow. But the bulk of the Spottiswoode lands was in Lammermuir, stretching almost to Longformacus, and their house stood 750 feet above sea level. Before the improvement of the estate in the eighteenth century, which is the subject of this book, it was a bleak, wild, windswept place, more fit for hunters than for agriculturalists. In *The Bride of Lammermuir*, Scott makes the seventeenth-century Ravenswood contemptuous of the fat farming lairds of the Merse. This is perhaps a chronoclasm by Sir Walter, for no lairds of the seventeenth century interested themselves overmuch in farming.

Nevertheless there may well have been rivalries between the lairds of Lammermuir and Merse, and on the strength of their record, the Spottiswoodes would doubtless have sided with the Ravenswoods of their time.

For if the sixteenth century was as lawless as the 14th, records were better. Brawling and feuding were still commonplace, but they did not always go unrecorded, or even always unpunished. The records of the Privy Council, which was the only source of central authority however limited its powers of enforcement, report that Spottiswoodes were either the perpetrators or victims of violence on at least six occasions between 1570 and the end of the century, and were twice 'denounced rebels'. It is true that in 1572 Ninian Spottiswoode of that Ilk was one of the Border lairds who put his name to an agreement to keep the peace of the Borders (Privy Council record of 12 Feb. 1572). But they were soon in trouble again. In 1594 William Spottiswoode of that Ilk was summoned to appear before the Privy Council to answer for the 'deadly feuds' he had entered into, a charge that implies that clan loyalties were strong. The results of these proceedings are unknown, but it is quite likely that they entailed some monetary penalties, in that age when there was so little cash in circulation. As will shortly appear, by the early seventeenth century the Laird of Spottiswoode professed himself a ruined man.

Time was not on the side of the Ravenswoods of history. But meanwhile there were other aspects of the Spottiswoodes more interesting than the brawling and threatening that were endemic in the Borders. This may be the time to note the credible report that a 14th-century Laird built a chapel, which is said to have stood, in whole or in part, until the 1770s or later. The Lairds of the golden age preferred to ignore the lawlessness associated with Spottiswoode of Spottiswoode, and it was fortunate that they, as saviours of the house, were able to claim a more reputable, if shorter, pedigree. They believed that their line began with a Spottiswoode who was killed at Flodden in 1513, although they could not quite agree on who he was. Lt. Col. George Spottiswoode of Gladswood, the Laird's brother, was conducting separate researches on the family in the 1840s (NLS MS 2923) and argued that the Spottiswoode slain at Flodden was Archibald, while the majority view seems to have been that he was William. The question of whether he was actually the Laird in possession is left vague. Whatever he was, they claimed that he was the father of a new kind of Spottiswoode, a scholar, and their own direct ancestor.

2

Spottiswoodes in Church and State

IN THE LANGUAGE of a seventeenth-century bishop, the supposed orphan of Flodden 'was no sword-man, but betook himself to the study of the Arts, passing his course of Philosophy in the College of Glasgow' (memoir of Archbishop of Spottiswoode printed with the latter's *History of the Church and State of Scotland*, published posthumously in 1655 and 1677; the memoir is in the name of Brian Duppa, Bishop of Winchester, although his authorship has been doubted). Duppa, if he was the author, took the young scholar's parentage on trust. He was certainly enrolled at Glasgow, but oddly, alone among his fellow entrants, his father's name and rank are not given. The nineteenth-century Spottiswoodes knew this, but their inability to prove a direct line from the earliest lairds of Spottiswoode was glossed over. It seems to have done nothing to diminish their family pride.

The student of Glasgow, John Spottiswoode (1510–1585), became a clergyman, and adhered to the cause of reform; he first came under the influence of Cranmer in England, and then of John Knox in Scotland, being presented to the living of Calder, where Knox was a visitor to Sir James Sandilands at Calder House. John Knox's short-lived scheme of church government required the appointment of superintendents, who were bishops in all but name. Spottiswoode was appointed Superintendent of the churches in Lothian, Tweeddale and the Merse, and held the office from 1560 to 1585. Superintendent Spottiswoode had two sons who became bishops. The elder, John, became Archbishop of Glasgow in James VI and I's revived and unpopular episcopalian church in Scotland, then Archbishop of St Andrews and Primus of Scotland, and finally Lord Chancellor. The younger, James, became Bishop of Clogher in Ireland.

The claim that the Superintendent John was directly descended from the lairds of Spottiswoode cannot be proved one way or the other, and from our point of view it is not important. These were new men of their own time, who raised the Spottiswoode family to a far higher level of eminence. But, even if they were descended from the House, they were not themselves lairds of Spottiswoode. The Lammermuir lairds of the Ravenswood type were obsolete, but they did not immediately disappear. The days of lawlessness on the Borders were coming to an end, hastened by the Union of the Crowns in 1603. The last years of Elizabeth's reign were marked by extreme violence among those Border hills that form Spottiswoode's southern horizon, and strenuous, ruthless and well-documented efforts by her administration to stamp it out. The Spottiswoodes of that Ilk did not raid over the Border, but they continued to behave in traditional ways. Matters came to a head in 1611 when John Spottiswoode of that Ilk was reported to the Privy Council for having killed a Lammermuir neighbour, Matthew Sinclair of Longformacus. Another looming feud between two landed families aroused the irritation of James VI and I, who told the Council in terse terms to get on and settle the matter quickly and not bother him further.

That the King was bothered at all was doubtless due to the presence on the Privy Council of the guilty party's kinsman, by now Archbishop of Glasgow. As we have seen, his degree of kinship cannot be definitely established, but he was certainly closely concerned. The Bishop set his seal on a covering letter to the King, pleading that the murder was not committed in cold blood but in 'chaudmella', from the French *chaude mêlée*, meaning a scuffle arising in the heat of passion. With the letter went an offer from the hot-blooded Laird, if the Laird he was, offering to pay compensation of a thousand merks to the widow and children of Matthew Sinclair. Written in the broadest Scots of the time, the offer is couched in piteous terms not only of remorse and regret, but of protestations of poverty. He reminded the Sinclairs of 'my awine hard estate querrof I zet again prayis thame, for Christis saik, to have pitie and consideration'; in short, the 1000 merks was more than he could afford, being 'altogidder broght to ruyne'. The Sinclairs seemed inclined to want him to face trial but as no more is heard of the matter they were presumably persuaded to take the money. The sum was not large, amounting to only about £30 sterling; but coin was in short supply.

None of the persons involved in this affair can be identified in the conventional but unreliable accounts of the families concerned, first given by Sir Robert Douglas in his *Baronage of Scotland* (1798) and more or less repeated, for the Spottiswoodes, in successive editions of *Burke's Landed Gentry*. This may not be from a wish to suppress a discreditable episode in the family history, but from genuine confusion. As already noted, the line of descent, or the line of possession, in those troubled generations is far from clear. One thing is clear, that the early seventeenth century was a turning point in the family, as in the country as a whole. The feuding lairds disappear from view, though they did not die off as neatly as the Douglas and Burke version have it. They are replaced centre-stage by three generations of remarkable men, of whom Archbishop John Spottiswoode was the most prominent in history. He was however also the means whereby the ancient estate passed, temporarily, out of the family.

Once again the sequence of events is obscure. Burke has it that the Archbishop, who was the son of the Superintendent and the grandson of the Spottiswoode who fell at Flodden, succeeded to the estate and representation of the family on the death of a cousin, another clergyman, in 1611, the very year of the affray between Spottiswoode and Sinclair. In that case what happened to the knife-pulling John Spottiswoode of that Ilk? Was he really so 'altogidder broght to ruyne' that he had to renounce his estate? There was only one man at that time who might bail out a Spottiswoode in trouble, namely the Archbishop. In the family papers there is evidence that he had a lien on the estate already in 1605. An inventory of deeds at Spottiswoode drawn up in a relatively modern hand (NLS MS 2936, ff. 193–201) includes an extract from a contract of that year between the Archbishop and John Spottiswoode 'then of that Ilk' showing that the former had, 'before the date of the sd Contract', paid the latter not 1000 merks but £1000 Scots. Ten years later, the incident with the Sinclairs having come and gone, it seems that the Archbishop foreclosed on his, perhaps, feckless kinsman. Producing the above contract, he obtained in August 1615 a renunciation of the lands of Spottiswoode in his favour 'seeing that the sd Archbishop had then and before advanced to him and his creditors great sumes of money'.

NLS MS 10285, f. 176 gives another account of these matters by a later Laird. It states 'in this year [1615] also he [the Archbishop] acquired the lands of Spottiswoode, Brotherfield etc. from John, son of Ninian as stated above page 7 on the 10th November and almost immediately i.e. by a deed of resignation executed on the 20th and 27th of the same month and with the consent of John Spottiswoode, his elder son, and also with consent of John Spottiswoode sometime of that Ilk, sold the same to Hugh, George and William Bell'. Unfortunately 'page 7 above' is not to be found.

This 'John Spottiswoode sometime of that Ilk' is likely to be the same who killed Matthew Sinclair. He was still alive in 1624 but his progeny never recovered the estate. Presumably they were absorbed into the larger family network. After several centuries the Spottiswoode name had already spread over many parts of southern Scotland and into Northumberland. It was not long before they went much further afield. The usual annals are only concerned with a few main lines, landed, professional or commercial, or all three. They say nothing of many others who bore the name of Spottiswoode, minor members of the clan, younger sons of younger sons, illegitimate offspring, servants who took the name of their master. These are all a problem to the genealogists, but need not be a problem to this narrative.

Archbishop John Spottiswoode (1565–1639) was the most eminent historical Spottiswoode. The son of the Superintendent, he followed his father to the living of Calder at an extremely young age, and apparently without ever being ordained. Even before his time as Lord Chancellor from 1635 to 1639, he was one of the most powerful men in Scotland, though he is remembered more as a churchman and historian than a man of action. His *History of the Church and State of Scotland*, first published posthumously in 1655, is still a source book for its period. His ideas and policies, as he moved from the Knoxian circle of his youth to an Erastian belief in the King's supremacy over the church, are well documented. His private life is less so. Spottiswoode seems to have been a worthy, rather than an out-and-out worldly man, but he had a certain state to maintain, and to be close to the throne was expensive as well as dangerous. His motives in the transactions just described can never be fully known. There is no record of what he obtained from the Bell brothers for the estate. Did he regard it as redundant? He had not been born nor lived there, and before the improvements of the next century there can have been little to covet in those windswept marshy acres. Besides, his duties lay elsewhere. The transaction took place within six months of his elevation to the see of St Andrews, and the following year, 1616, he bought the former episcopal estate at Dairsie, just a few miles to the west of St Andrews, which he promptly vested in his elder son, John. It might be argued that he showed by his actions that he was not after all of the direct line, but this does not necessarily follow. He must have been above all a pragmatist.

The religious politics in which Archbishop Spottiswoode played a leading role were as complicated as they were dangerous, and are thankfully outside the scope of this Introduction. It was the misfortune of himself and the family to be historically on the wrong side. If his side had won, he might have founded a dynasty comparable to the greatest Border or Fife families. Before disaster overtook them, this must have seemed well on the way. His elder son John was established at Dairsie, where the Archbishop improved the castle and built a church. Sir Robert Spottiswoode, the younger son, was likewise on the way to a settled landed future, and also became a legal and political luminary in the royalist tradition of his father. He had acquired the old monastic estate of New Abbey near Dumfries in 1624, only to be obliged to surrender it to the King in 1634 to provide an income for the newly created Bishopric of Edinburgh (which his father had instigated), in return for a worthless promise of £3000 sterling. Instead he acquired Dunipace in Stirlingshire and took his title, as a judge, from that. For some reason he sold it in

1643, but it returned to the family at some time and was the seat of a branch of the family in the eighteenth and nineteenth centuries.

The Spottiswoodes' connection with Dairsie proved to be short-lived. But what the Archbishop did there is too interesting to be passed over. There is a persistent belief that he turned the castle into something luxurious and French, which seems to have no other basis than the rumours put about by his Presbyterian enemies, who did not hesitate to ascribe the most unlikely immoralities to him. As it happens, Dairsie Castle has undergone a radical restoration by a private owner, but not before a careful archaeological investigation was made. No evidence has been found that it was ever any larger than the surviving modestly sized ruin, and it appears never to have had any defensive outworks. Spottiswoode seems to have added some upperworks, in the manner of Claypotts, but otherwise his transformation, if it amounted to that, must have been confined to the interior, where some fragments of a floor of imported marble have been found. More interesting is the discovery that he made a simple little Renaissance garden under the castle wall on a terrace overlooking the River Eden, with a tiny oval pavement and riggs or beds for flowers and herbs. Perhaps even that was enough to inflame the dislike of the Presbyterians.

As to the church, his biographer, in England and not knowing the local situation, recorded that 'he publicly, and upon his own charges, built and adorned the Church of Darsey after the decent English form; which, if the boisterous hand of a mad Reformation hath not disordered, is at this time one of the beautifullest little pieces of church-work that is left to that now unhappy country'. The structure of Dairsie in fact survived, although the interior, on which Spottiswoode had lavished so much care, was indeed 'disordered' and has all been replaced. He designed it to be an ideal frame for what he thought the episcopal service in Scotland should be: sober, dignified and informed by grace, and not at all Popish as the opposing party asserted. The exterior was of lesser importance, but it is interesting that Spottiswoode chose a rough version of the English decorated style (the 'decent English form'), with plate tracery windows that are, alas, very crudely executed.

Dairsie church was an early example of the fundamental wish to unite the various strands of the reformed Episcopalian faith, which in later centuries became so typical of Anglicanism. For the west door Spottiswoode chose a Renaissance idiom with flanking pilasters, bearing the date 1621 and surmounted by his arms in a strapwork cartouche, all small and not very skilful but the necessary building skills must have been hard to come by. Dr Marinell Ash (in *Scottish Church History Records*, 1976, xix, pt.2) thinks that this door was modelled on the door of the Chapel Royal at Stirling Castle (1594), but that is a bold, full-blown triumphal arch in the Palladian manner, while Dairsie is in a timid English Jacobethan. Here, as in his little garden, Spottiswoode was trying to cultivate some modest flowers of social and religious civility in a hostile environment. He did not put up his own motto on his armorial, but the words *Dilexi Decorem Domus Tuae*, from Psalm 26 v.8, 'I have loved the beauty [A.V. 'the habitation'] of thy house'.

3

The Shadow of the Maiden

THESE FLOWERS were all rudely plucked out, for the Spottiswoodes and for their country, by the stark iconoclasm of the time in Scotland. Following the riots that accompanied the introduction of the Laudian prayerbook in 1637, and the triumph of Presbyterianism in 1638, Scotland became too dangerous for Archbishop Spottiswoode. He did not live to see the final shipwreck of his King in the Civil War, since he died in late 1639 and was buried with pomp and ceremony in Westminster Abbey. Archbishop Spottiswoode was fortunate to die a natural death with full honours. Not all his descendants were so lucky. The younger son, Robert, who achieved almost the eminence of his father, paid for it with his life. After his brother's execution at St Andrews in 1647, the elder son John left Dairsie. Contrary to what is often written, it was not he but his son, yet another John, who was executed with Montrose in 1650. The father John retired to Northumberland, dying in obscurity at Newcastle in 1677, but leaving sons who, the family account says, became farmers (NLS MS 2936). The Dairsie estate was acquired by the Morison family of Preston-grange, the family of his sister-in-law Bethia, Sir Robert's wife.

As the children of the Archbishop's elder son effectively left the scene, the preservation of the main line of Spottiswoode, as it now was, devolved on the children of Sir Robert. Like his father's, Sir Robert's life is well known to history. He too became a favourite of James VI and I, who knighted him and made him a Privy Councillor at the age of 27 or 28. His rise continued under Charles I. As President of the Court of Session after 1633, he became hateful to the Presbyterian party, and like his father had to flee when they triumphed in 1638. But unlike his father, Sir Robert returned to Scotland. Charles was able to protect him for a while but finally gave him the kiss of death by appointing him Secretary of State in 1643 and charging him to deliver a Royal Warrant to Montrose, whom the Scots regarded as a rebel. Captured after Montrose's defeat at Philiphaugh in 1645, he paid the price at St Andrews in January 1646, meeting his death with other distinguished Royalists under the Maiden, Scotland's primitive guillotine.

The manner of Sir Robert's death, too, is well known. The story goes that he was prevented from exercising the usual privilege of a last speech, but was able to hand on its script, which was later printed. Among the more precious possessions of later Spottiswoodes was a letter he wrote to his young children on the eve of his execution, together with a list of all the children his wife had borne him (some of whom had died in infancy), the day and hour of their birth, and whom they had been named after. As far as I can see the original has not survived, but several copies were made, one of which landed up in Virginia, as we shall see. As it is short, the letter can be quoted in full:

My Dear Children

It is Gods pleasure that you be deprived of me, who I trust will not be wanting to supply my loss to you another way especially if you seek him earnestly which I beg of him that you may. My brother for the present will have a care of you, until the country be quieted I have left the charge of you chiefl y to him as nearest to me, and I doubt not but kindest to you. Your grandmother uncle and friends of your mothers side I enjoin you to honour and respect and ye laird of [word illegible] and Mr John Scougal as much as any; who if I be not mistaken will give place to none for kindness and good advice. All that I have to bequeath you is the example of my loyalty: which as you look for a blessing from heaven or will have mind to light upon you I command you to imitate and never to set your faces against your prince for any cause whatsoever. I hope you shall sustain neither infamy nor prejudice by this death of mine if you are not wanting to your selves (of course?) ? present my last goodnight

Sir Robert Spottiswoode's death ended the eminence of the Spottiswoode family in Scottish affairs, and although his son Alexander is said to have retained the favour of Charles II, and even to have been with him in hiding in England, royal negligence and the continued tension in Scotland between the Crown, the Kirk and the landed interest ensured that there was little to show for it. If Sir Robert had died in possession of Spottiswoode, it would have been forfeited as it is sometimes said it was, but he did not. The Spottiswoodes' great dispute with the Crown did not concern Spottiswoode but New Abbey. The already-mentioned £3000 sterling, in typical Stuart fashion, was never paid. After the bishops were turned out in 1638, Charles I put his signature to a paper restoring Sir Robert's title to the estate (and withdrawing the promised £3000). Obviously this was of no effect in Sir Robert's lifetime, but after the Restoration his son Alexander profited from his closeness to Charles II if only to the extent of getting a new Charter from him, and possessed the estate, at least in theory, from 1660 to 1662. But in that year an Act was passed restoring the bishops and the lands that had been held by their predecessors in 1637. So the Spottiswoodes were once again out, and the £3000 was again promised. 'But neither was the said sum . . . payed, nor any part of far greater sums that were due by King Charles 1st to my grandfather.' These words are from a printed broadsheet of 1695 (NLS 7.70 [19]), almost certainly from his own press, setting out a petition by John Spottiswoode to be restored to the estate of New Abbey. John Spottiswoode (of whom presently, as the genealogists say) was the son of Alexander and grandson of the executed Sir Robert.

Alexander Spottiswoode occupies an interesting place in the history of the family. He was a boy when his father was killed, and brought up thereafter by his maternal uncle, Sir Alexander Morison of Prestongrange. In 1682 the elderly Sir Alexander was fined for permitting 'tumult and disorder' at Prestonpans Church when a nominee of the Bishop of Edinburgh was to preach there. He protested to the Privy Council at being penalised for something he could not prevent, and cited his loyalty to the Crown in the time of Charles I, and his respect for his brother-in-law Sir Robert Spottiswoode, whose children he had had to educate. He stated that Sir Robert's grandchild by his eldest son was presently (1682) in his family and being 'intertained by him at schooles'. As a result, the Duke of York introduced a resolution in the Privy Council that the grandchildren of Sir Robert Spottiswoode 'who are now in necessity' should be supplied out of the fine imposed on the heritors of Preston.

All this is very odd. As we have seen, Sir Robert's children can be accounted for, and his eldest son John (b.1630) is said in the family trees to have died unmarried before 1660, in which case, even if he had had illegitimate children, they would have been in their twenties. The next son was Alexander who had died in 1675 and who, having been married twice to daughters of landed families, should not have left his children unprovided for. The third son, Robert, may well have been the worst sufferer from his father's execution, or perhaps his uncle's generosity could not extend very far in his case. But in 1682 he was an Army Surgeon in Tangier and his only son, the future Governor of Virginia, was with him. It seems that Morison must have been referring to John, the son of Alexander by his second marriage, of whom much more later, who would have been about 16 in 1682. Why he should have been 'in necessity' remains a mystery.

4

The Family Fortunes Revive

W E SHALL have to leave this puzzle concerning the Spottiswoodes at this point in their fortunes, and return to Alexander. We have seen the family in two distinct phases, each related to a broad band of Scottish history. First came the generations of hot-blooded Lammermuir lairds with their feuding kinsmen and tacksmen. During the century when religious affairs were of paramount importance, Spottiswoodes rose to the highest positions in the church. Their failure to rise again after the Restoration reflected the Stuarts' failure to reimpose episcopacy peacefully. The settlement in favour of Presbyterianism, which followed William and Mary's accession in 1688, took the heat out of the situation and allowed the landed interest to reach an understanding with the established Kirk. There were to be no more ecclesiastical grandees; what the landed interest wanted were ministers, neither too grand nor too humble, to preach the established order, in which they took rank well under the heritors of the parish. It was time for the Spottiswoodes, at least those who were not able or willing to live off their land holdings, to find other means to maintain or advance their standing.

Alexander did not have possession of the family estate during his quite short lifetime, but as we have seen, he briefly had New Abbey. He took the territorial title 'of Crumstaine' from his first wife's Home estate near Duns, to which she was sole heiress. Presumably he lived there from time to time. But really he was an Edinburgh man. He had foreseen that the profession of the future was the law. It is true that his father, Sir Robert, had been a law man and had written a book about the practice of law in Scotland, but he was so bound up in the affairs of church and court that he is unrecognisable as a lawyer in the modern sense. If the new governing landed class had little use for ambitious clergy, they had a constant need for lawyers to manage their affairs and fight their legal battles. These lawyers were largely drawn from their own class, and soon began to form almost a class within a class, so rich were their opportunities to acquire property. It is a truism that after the Union of the Parliaments in 1707 the real government of Scotland were the lawyers.

True to this vision of the future, Alexander Spottiswoode became one of the first of the profession of advocate as we know it. King Charles II was still on the throne and it was still possible for the legal profession to come into conflict with arbitrary power. Although he was described by the later family as 'a firm friend of the Royal Family' (*Burke's Landed Gentry*), he appears not to have been a sycophant. In 1674 he was one of the advocates charged to quit Edinburgh for not remaining at the Bar, and not permitted to come within twelve miles of the City unless they petitioned the Lords of Session for readmission. He and others signed a humble address to the Privy Council on the subject, for which boldness they were prohibited from leaving the country before 15 March 1676. But while this ban was still in force, Alexander died, at the age of 44.

Alexander Spottiswoode's legal career was the beginning of a new phase in the history of the family, but he died before the disappearance of Stuart arbitrary power and the religious settlement of 1689 marked the beginning of the modern history of Scotland. On a personal level, little is known about him. Some of the family papers in the National Library which seem to have no direct connection with Spottiswoode may be fragments of his professional archive. As a youth he was uncertain both of his profession and his marriage, for one of the papers (in NLS MS 2933) is a long exhortation to him from an older friend on these subjects. As already noted, he was married twice, first to the only daughter of Sir John Home of Crumstaine, and secondly to Helen Trotter of Mortonhall. His reported only son by the first marriage is said by Burke, who does not name him, to have died unmarried. Presumably this son also died young, for his half-brother John, Helen Trotter's child, was the one who took up Alexander's claim to the estate of New Abbey. During the first, unsuccessful

hearing of John's petition of 1695 to be restored to New Abbey, we find
him named, perhaps incorrectly, as Mr John Spottiswoode of Crumstaine.
After this, however, the Spottiswoode connection with Crumstaine seems
to have ceased.

John Spottiswoode's petition of 1695 to be restored to the estate of
New Abbey failed, apparently because the advisers to William and Mary
preferred the revenues to go to the Kirk in Dumfries. It may have been
this failure that determined him to get back the old family estate. By
succeeding in doing so, he became the founder of the modern landed
family. He was the first of the four successive John Spottiswoodes of that
Ilk who ruled the estate during what I have called its golden age, and
whom it is convenient here to call Johns I to IV.

After the Archbishop and his son Robert, John I was the Spottiswoode
best known in his own time, through his large practice as an advocate,
by which professional name he is always known – 'John Spottiswoode
the Advocate'. He was also known to later generations as the author of
a life of Sir Robert which was prefaced to the latter's *Practicks of the Law
of Scotland*, published in an edition of 1706. This became a text for the
later historians of the family, and it is also a kind of declaration in favour
of the Spottiswoodes and their claim to ancient lineage and royal favour.
As such its objectivity is suspect, as we may see from the grandiloquent
opening:

> Spottiswoode . . . was never known to have been in the Possession of any
> other Family or Surname, except that it has been near a hundred years past,
> in the Property of some Portioners no way related to the Spottiswoods.
> But GOD (who in his appointed time will restore every person and family
> to their Right) has Blessed the endeavours of John Spotiswood Sir Robert's
> Grandchild, and enabled him to recover this Ancient Inheritance of his
> Predecessors.

John I goes on to express pious hopes that God will move the Royal
Family to make restitution and suitable reward for his family's services,
and reparation for their manifest losses:

But notwithstanding the Traverses of Fortune, and the want of a warm influence from the Throne, the Spotiswoods have maintained their Primitive Character, and purpose to follow Vertue for Vertue's sake, seeing it is a sufficient reward to itself.

John Spottiswoode I was born in 1666, the son of Alexander's second wife, Helen Trotter of Mortonhall, south of Edinburgh. He is the first Spottiswoode of whom it is possible to form some sort of personal picture from the family papers, fragmentary as they are. John received a long and rigorous training in the law from Edinburgh University and in the chambers of his relative James Hay, a prominent Writer and Conveyancer, to whom his mother had indentured him. Among the surviving papers in the National Library are several of his notebooks, which in their tiny format and crabbed writing suggest a canny man. He made them serve for recording many things, from receipts of fees, payments to his mother or sister, his trips from Edinburgh to Berwickshire, his laundry, down to the movement of his bowels. John I seems to have been a bit of a perpetual student, for in 1705, when he was nearly forty, he noted down a systematic programme of reading and study, written in both English and Latin, and including works on geometry, arithmetic, trigonometry, logic, metaphysics and mythology. Many of the entries are written in French; NLS MS 2947 begins in 1697 with a resolution to take notes of the affairs of the day *chaque soir avant coucher* (sic). This practice of writing in French adds an extra touch of ambiguity to the entry (13th January 1702): *Jaques Spotswood mon garcon est entre apprentis au Jean Cheyne apoticaire a Leyth.* Is this another skeleton in the family cupboard? English sufficed to record in 1701 that 'Andrew Spotswood my late servant was bound apprentice to Jo. Vallenge'. 'Garcon' or 'servant', it is impossible to know what precisely is meant by these terms. But whatever their relationship to the family, these young men both bore the name of Spottiswoode.

Vallenge was a bookseller, and perhaps also a printer and publisher, in Edinburgh. He provided a poste-restante for Spottiswoode, for example the letters from his cousin in Virginia were directed via Vallenge. So the 'servant' Andrew may well be the same who became a bookseller in Durham (information from Mrs Dorothy Dore) and who directed begging letters to John II about the year 1740 (Edinburgh University Library).

The bookish connection was already, and was to become even more, important to the Spottiswoodes. When Archbishop Spottiswoode was writing his *History*, he assembled a mass of material from Scotland and abroad, in which his son Robert was said to have assisted him. He specifically left his books to Robert, but his library is supposed to have been destroyed when he had to flee Scotland in 1638. Many, however, were in the possession of Sir Alexander Dick of Prestonfield in the middle of the eighteenth century, and after him, Sir George Warrender, and were published in two volumes by the Scottish History Society in 1931/2. It seems quite probable that others remained with his descendants. The dissenting Minister of Stichill, George Ridpath, in spite of his Presbyterianism, was familiar with Spottiswoode and refers to staying there, to reading the Archbishop's *History* and checking it against a manuscript, which must therefore have been in John II's possession (*Diary of George Ridpath, 1755–61*, Scottish History Society series 3, vol 2, 1922).

Whether or not any books reached the Archbishop's great-grandson John I, the latter certainly amassed an enormous library of his own. A little-known catalogue (NLS B.C.5.1) reveals that John's library was put on sale in Edinburgh on 1st July 1728, a short time after his death. It lists about 2000 items, of which the majority were in Latin or European languages. Perhaps the size of his library has something to do with the law school that John conducted. He is sometimes said to have been the first Professor of Law at Edinburgh University, although I have come across no claim of his own to that title. In fact, as an Episcopalian he would have been excluded from a University chair, and he seems to have been but one of a number of men at the time who might have expected such recognition and never received it. In connection with his teaching and practice he was also a prolific writer of law manuals. As an advocate, he was best known, and in some quarters hated, for his defence of the Captain and crew of the English ship *Worcester*, who were victims of a miscarriage of justice when they were accused of piracy in the Indian Ocean, but in reality were made scapegoats for the confiscation of the Darien Company's last ship by the East India Company. Spottiswoode conducted a vigorous defence which was acknowledged by Captain Green in his last speech; it was not however sufficient to save Green from the gallows, and it exposed Spottiswoode to a lot of partisan hatred. He emerges as a good guy in an episode that does contemporary Scotland no credit.

5

The Recovery
of Spottiswoode

A S THE GRANDSON of the beheaded Sir Robert, John was still to
some extent in the shadows, and it was his preoccupation to escape
from them and to restore the family name. As we have seen, the circumstances of his upbringing are obscure, and if he was not actually poor he
may well have been very dependent. His notebooks show that he tried
to budget his expenditure to the last penny. They also show an unashamed
desire to improve his social position: he reminds himself 'to seek after
the acquaintance of the young nobility, and insinuate myself into th'
antienter sort'. This does not seem the attitude of a man confident of his
lineage. Today we would expect that he should be proud to be the
great-grandson of the Archbishop and grandson of a martyred Royalist
grandee, but in the new climate of Presbyterianism and Whiggery it was
not a recommendation, and as we have seen in his dealings with the
University, it excluded him from the ascendant establishment of the day.
At the end of the life of his grandfather, already quoted, John makes a
plea for moderation and mutual tolerance, for, he writes:

> the Difference betwixt these of the Episcopal Persuasion and those of the
> Presbyterian, lyes in matters of very small moment to Salvation, and con-
> cern only the external Government of Churchmen, wherein the Laity have
> no concern.

John I's anxiety to restore the family fortunes is most explicit in his
correspondence with his cousin Alexander Spottiswoode, his father's

younger brother's son, the Governor of Virginia. The correspondence, preserved at Williamsburg, began in 1696, when Alexander was an officer in the English army, stationed in Sudbury in Suffolk before going to the Low Countries, and ended in 1724 when Alexander had already been replaced as Governor of Virginia and was in London negotiating the settlement of his affairs. It was a somewhat one-sided correspondence, for John was a reluctant and sporadic letter-writer, and although they met once before it began, they were never to meet again. When John did write, he was direct enough: 'let both of us, who are the only males of the family Spotswood, endeavour with a noble emulation to render it once more conspicuous . . . I beg you'd take care of yourself, and govern your courage with your prudence, for on your life contains that of half of the family' (letter of January 1704/5. John had just heard that Alexander had been wounded at the Battle of Blenheim, but had survived).

Alexander's was a classic colonial success story; as well as holding the office of Lieutenant Governor of Virginia (the actual office of Governor was a sinecure) from 1710 to 1722, he became a huge landowner and an ironmaster, and must for his time have been the richest living Spottiswoode. John I certainly thought so, and said so in a letter. In 1711 John tried to interest him in buying back the estate of Dairsie, which was then on the market. But Alexander was not yet rich enough to commit the £6,000 Sterling purchase price when the course of his life was not clear to him. John was disappointed, but he knew that Alexander, who was still unmarried, intended to leave his fortune to the Scottish family. That was apparently still the case in 1723. However, in 1724 Alexander came to London to establish his title to his Virginian estates, and while there he married and started a family of his own. In fact he stayed in London for six years, during which time John Spottiswoode I died in Scotland. The New World was not after all to redress the balance of the Old.

All this time, however, John I had not been idle himself in restoring the family fortunes. He had the proceeds of his law practice, his law school, and the sales of his prolific legal textbooks, besides whatever he drew from the estate or other property. In 1695 he petitioned the Crown for the restitution of the New Abbey estate, but failed, as we have already seen. Meanwhile, his notebooks show that he was in the habit of going to Thornydykes, a barony adjacent to Spottiswoode, where lived his sister Janet and her husband George Brown. It was from there that in 1700 he negotiated the repurchase of the ancient estate from the family to which the archbishop had sold it. In 1710 he made a good marriage, to Helen Arbuthnott, daughter of Viscount Arbuthnott and widow of the chief of the clan Macfarlane. His heir, John II, the central character of this book, was born in 1711. Nothing is known of the condition of Spottiswoode when John I repossessed it. It is a fair assumption that it was neglected and unimproved, if not actually ruinous. There must have been an old tower of some sort, such as every border estate possessed, which may or may not have been enlarged according to the still primitive notions of the sixteenth or seventeenth century. There is some evidence that it was still standing in the early nineteenth century but no drawing of it is known to me.

It is frustrating that John I never referred to his improvements at Spottiswoode in his correspondence with Alexander. The latter was a famous builder, who was responsible not only for the palatial Governor's mansion so carefully replicated by Colonial Williamsburg, but for an extensive country house at Germanna in his county of Spotsylvania, which was finished by 1732 but stood for a mere 50 years. John I too was building, though there is precious little evidence of the fact. What he built sufficed for the family for 130 years. I have seen the careful excavations of the foundations of Governor Spotswood's 'enchanted palace' (in the words of a contemporary), conducted by Mary Washington College, Fredericksburg. I could not help thinking then of those other foundations lying unknown and undisturbed under a few feet, even a few inches, of Berwickshire turf – the dateless old tower, the ancient chapel, the house that John I built, the huge William IV mansion built by John IV. It is time that archaeology in this country too addressed itself to such sites, which are now as remote from us in imagination as any bronze age burial mound, if rather more interesting.

When John IV built his great house in the 1830s, the existing house was, unusually, not pulled down. It was remodelled and the larger house attached to its southwestern corner. In the photographs of the later house, used in the sale catalogues of 1919 and 1935, the western end of the older one can be seen, obviously clothed in stonework by the later architect. I have seen only one small photograph of the front, showing that it had been a manageable house of three storeys, five well-spaced windows wide. Clearly it was already very different from the house of the early 1700s, but it is not clear how many changes it had undergone. We know that John II made additions and improvements, which may have included adding a third storey.

There is no record of when John I started to build, but in 1705 he was buying timber at Leith to be sent to Spottiswoode (NLS MS 2947). The following year he may or may not have had a new house, but he had a garden, for he made a list of seeds to be sent there, including onions, leeks, carrots, parsnips, lettuce, beetroot, spinach and radishes. These were to be 'sent to Spotswood [sic] Garden for my own use', while a more limited selection was to go to the gardener's wife. So Spottiswoode was already being civilised. The existence of a kitchen garden certainly implies well-established shelter, either by high walls or planting or both. It is a pity that John I did not record the source of his seeds, but it may well have been the John Arro who supplied vegetables to Dalkeith Palace in 1702–03 (A. Hope: *A Caledonian Feast*, 1987, p.177). The sophistication of the list supports Mrs Hope's observation that despite the reputation of the Scots for not eating vegetables, the Scottish gentry were at least as fond of them as their English counterparts, except perhaps in the Highlands. Still, it is doubtful whether John I's quick-on-the-draw forebears would have spent time on cultivating spinach.

But what of the house that John built? As to that there is only one small clue. Either John I or John II, having a house, wished to lay out its surroundings in a suitable manner. Three rudimentary plans for a formal layout are known, one of which includes a tiny elevation of a house. It shows a typical manor house of the period when fortification was no longer necessary, but small windows and thick walls persisted as a style of building. As far as one can see it had a pantiled roof, which pressed down close against the upper windows. As it has five window bays, it is reasonable to suppose that this is indeed the house which survived to be encased and added to John IV's mansion. It was not a grand house with classical detail, but a plain laird's house like, for example, Newton House at Millerhill.

6

The Laird in Possession

JOHN SPOTTISWOODE I died in 1728, leaving his heir John II as a minor. John II is the *raison d'être* and hero of this book, since the diary, estate ledger, call it what you will, discussed here, covers the management of the estate during most of his long life as Laird. It does not begin until more than 20 years after he reached his majority in 1732, and there are references in it to a preceding book which has not come to light. So we do not know exactly when he assumed the management of the estate, or what he did before doing so. Probably, as with all members of the family at this time, he was a great deal in Edinburgh. By his own account 'my friends took care to educate me in the profession of the family viz the Law but I never entered upon the Practise'. In 1740 John married Mary Thomson, the daughter of another legal family who had an estate in Fife, who was to bear him eight children. A touching relic of this event may be found in the National Library (NLS 1937.13 [20]), a broadsheet printed at the top 'MARRIAGE is Honourable', with a primitive woodcut of a couple hand in hand. It has been filled in in ink with an 'Epithalamium' on the marriage of the 'Honourable Learned Judicious most Charitable well accomplished and highly renowned Honourable John Spotswood of that Ilk' to Miss Mary Thomson, daughter of the Hon. Mr John Thomson of Charletown, 'famous writer to His Majesties Signet'. There follow many lines of doggerel and hyperbole, dated 29 March 1740, two days after the marriage. The anonymous author of this drivel has appended the words 'let me know if this may be printed and published'. As there is no printed copy among the papers, we may hope that John II had better sense than to allow it.

If John II did not immediately bring his bride to live at Spottiswoode, the reason may lie elsewhere in Scotland. The recovery of the estate of New Abbey in the Stewartry of Kirkcudbright had been an obsession of the family since the restoration of King Charles II. Where his grandfather and father had failed, John II finally succeeded, and obtained a charter from King George II in 1742. By November that year he had carried out a careful survey of every part of his new property. The result is recorded in twelve beautifully ruled and written folios (NLS MS 2950). The entries are divided into four main columns, showing the rental payable on each property before the purchase of the estate by Sir Robert Spottiswoode, the rental payable to Sir Robert, to the Bishop of Edinburgh between 1662 and 1689, and finally the rents now due to John II. As the estate had not been in hand for half a century, changes had to be made, and matters were carefully noted as 'to be enquired into'. Lapses had to be investigated and squatters dispossessed. Many of the notes are written in the first person, and the warning *Nota* is often to be seen, just as in the Spottiswoode diary.

At New Abbey, as at Spottiswoode, John II was evidently a hands-on landlord. Yet it is not clear how much he lived there, when, or how long. In 1745 he was at Spottiswoode, receiving accounts from Edinburgh of the occupation of the city by Prince Charles's forces (NLS MS 2933, f. 65). In 1747 he wrote from New Abbey to Governor Spotswood's executor in Virginia. As late as 1764 he successfully pressed a claim against the Marquess of Tweeddale for the feus of the Parish of Baro in East Lothian, which had anciently been attached to New Abbey, and obtained a payment from the marquess for their redemption (NLS MS 14755, f. 105). Even in 1773 he was still pursuing the Crown on account of the broken promises of the previous century. But long before this, if we can judge from the diary, he was apparently in constant touch with the conduct of the Spottis-woode estate.

I have not yet found out why, or even when, John II disposed of the New Abbey estate. The date should be discoverable, but the motives may remain unclear. There may not have been a suitable house on the estate. The family interests were in Edinburgh and London, and New Abbey was less well placed for either than Spottiswoode, though as he pointed out to his American cousin, it was well placed for trade by sea with the American colonies. Whatever the course of events, when the Earl of Buchan received a letter from the elderly John II in 1786, he endorsed it as from 'John Spottiswode of Spottiswoode formerly of New Abbey' (EUL [Edinburgh University Library] LA II 588). And when John IV died in 1866, there was no reference to New Abbey in his Will. The Spottiswoodes seem to have left no trace of their presence in later accounts of the Parish.

So what sort of picture can we form of John Spottiswoode II? On the strength of the diary discussed here, he must count as the great improving laird of the family, although the greater wealth of his grandson brought about much more conspicuous changes to the estate. Between John II and his grandson John IV came John III, who had a successful career as a lawyer in the Inner Temple, and who ushers in a new and more cosmopolitan phase in the family history. It is possible that later generations tended to look back at John II as a bit of a primitive, more of a farmer than a gentleman laird. However, a portrait of him, recently discovered, gives a different impression, more in keeping with his scholarly tastes. The portrait is neither signed nor dated, but has been attributed to William Denune, and was probably a marriage portrait. A portrait of Mary Thomson, now at Charleton, may be its companion piece. As Denune practised in Dumfries, it is extra evidence that John II was at New Abbey around the time of his marriage.

Although his portrait depicts a polished gentleman, there is evidence that even in his own time John II was regarded by the up-and-coming as an old-fashioned man, a Scots laird of the old school. He himself wrote in 1745: 'Any interest [i.e. influence] I have is but very small for I live in a private way not meddling with publick affairs'. This was a prudent statement in 1745. John II was neither a stay-at-home nor an ignoramus. On Sunday 13th March 1763 James Boswell, in London, recorded that 'the afternoon was passed round the fire by Macfarlane, myself, Erskine and the Laird of Spottiswoode, a very curious exhibition. He is quite a braid-Scots man, his conversation was diverting from being so very unlike anything that I have heard for a good time. He is half brother to Macfarlane, and they have a great similarity. They are both crammed with knowledge of families and places in Scotland, and have both a sort of greasy drollery' (*Boswell's London Journal 1762–63*, 1950 ed., p. 215).

This unflattering description, had they ever heard it, would have been unwelcome to John IV and his daughter Alicia Anne, Lady John Scott, the *grande dame* of Spottiswoode in its final period. But we must put it in its context, for Boswell, who came from a similar background to Spottiswoode, was at this time trying his best to be a London sophisticate and as anglified as possible. Some of the description rings true enough, but as far as it includes Macfarlane it is flatly contradicted by other testimony. Walter Macfarlane was the Chief of the Clan, and was indeed John II's half-brother, his mother Helen Arbuthnott having married John I as her second husband. He has been described as one of the most laborious and accurate antiquaries of his age, and 'conspicuous for the utmost urbanity, and for his acquaintance with all the more elegant and especially antiquarian departments of literature'. The Faculty of Advocates bought his manuscripts in 1785, and the genealogical papers were published in two volumes by the Scottish History Society in 1900 as *Macfarlane's Genealogical Collections*. These conflicting views of the half-brothers, taken together, give a vivid picture of the conversation between these men on that March afternoon in 1763. They are also evidence, if we need it, that John II was in London from time to time, and had a circle among the Scottish gentry there.

John II may not have been an antiquary in the same league as his half-brother Macfarlane, but he had interests outside the improvement of his land. There is a persistent tradition in the family that he and his descendants were not merely Episcopalians but Jacobites. The loyalty of Episcopalians to the Hanoverian crown was always suspect, and there was a close connection between the Episcopalian and Jacobite causes in the Presbyterian mind. Historically the Spottiswoodes had reason, for the Archbishop and his son had risen, though they had also suffered, in the Stuart cause. In practical terms they had little to thank the Stuarts for, having failed to recover their estates under either Charles II or James VII

& II, whereas they prospered under the Hanoverians. By the time of the '15 and the '45, it would have spelt instant ruin for a landowner in the eastern Borders, whose gates lay on the high road to England, to declare openly for the Pretender. As noted, John II was at Spottiswoode in 1745, living 'in a private way', and there is no record of his having dealings with either side.

There are two pieces of possible evidence that the family did indeed harbour a secret attachment to the lost cause. The first is their possession at some date of a Jacobite glass, sold in 1991 with a Spottiswoode provenance. This is admittedly slim evidence, and there is no knowing if John himself owned the glass. It is much more likely that it came into the possession of the family in Lady John Scott's time, possibly from her mother's family the Wauchopes. This is the conclusion of Mrs Dorothy Dore, who has researched the authenticity of the claim made for the 'Amen' glass, sold for a high price to the Drambuie company. The second piece of evidence is a hitherto unnoticed scrap of writing among the family papers, bearing a rabidly Jacobite poem of four verses (NLS 2933, f. 79). It is not signed, but someone has written beneath it in very small letters the word 'Spottiswoode'. Whoever wrote the poem was not much of a poet, but was a man of sententious opinions. John II was such a man. To be sure, if this was really written in 1732, he was only 20 or 21, but the partisan tone suits that well enough. So perhaps this really is a youthful indiscretion by him; there are other verses among the papers that suggest a literary bent. Here are the first two verses:

June 10th, 1732. An Ode

Now Muse in gratefull numbers pay
Thy annuall tribute to this day.
First blest by injur'd James's Birth
And after more propitious grown
Snatched an Usurper from the Throne
Whose carcase stains not British Earth

Auspicious Day! Conclude again

> A second George's hated reign
> Now gone towards his native soil
> And if a Frederick shall succeed
> In the same Course with him proceed
> Remove such vermine from our isle.

The reason why June 10th, 'White Rose Day', was or is an auspicious day for Jacobites is that James Stuart, the 'old pretender', was born that day; and it grew 'more propitious' when George I had a seizure on June 10th 1727 and died two days later at Osnabruck. As the first verse implies, he was buried at Hanover, not in Britain. Thus far the poem makes sense, but there seems no record of George II visiting his native soil, presumably meaning Hanover, in 1732. Perhaps someone can put me right about this.

Anyone who knows Spottiswoode as a place must know the half-effaced inscriptions which flank the archway leading into the estate from the A697, and are found on several of the field gates between there and the entrance to the policies. In an unsigned drawing book, probably of the nineteenth century and considerably later than the stones themselves, somebody has transcribed the verses and drawn and named the arches and gates in which they were set. Thanks to that, we know that there were twelve of them altogether. Six are still *in situ*, three have been taken to the neighbouring farm of Blythe for their own safety, and three have disappeared.

These verses are often thought to be by Lady John Scott, who is known to have been a poet, and who is the lady of Spottiswoode whose name everybody remembers. In fact their style and sentiments are surely of an earlier age, for example:

> Since fleeting life so soon must end
> What can our vain pursuits intend
> From shore to shore why should we roam
> When none can leave himself at home

Or:

> Receive my council and securely move
> Intrust thy fortune to the powers above

Leave them to manage for thee & to grant
What their unerring wisdom sees thee want
In goodness and in greatness they excell
Ah! that we lov'd ourselves but half so well

These are still *in situ* and decipherable. Some that are now invisible or illegible convey still better this strange mixture of oppressive paternalism, fatalism and scepticism:

Those years which God bestows with thanks imploy
Nor long defer the bliss thou mayest enjoy
For so its pleasure and not change of air
That renders life a blessing anywhere
Those that beyond seas go will sadly find
They change the Climate only not the mind

It was unusual, to say the least, for a landowner to scatter sermons in stones along a mile of road, and although Lady John Scott would certainly have been eccentric enough to do it, it is far more likely that they were the work of her great-grandfather, John II. Their blend of sententiousness and learning, with a certain amount of primitive simplicity, fits our picture of the man.

Mr Barry has noted that the account of Westruther by the Parish minister, published in 1799 as part of the great Statistical Account of Scotland but possibly written in John II's lifetime, has nothing to say about the Spottiswoode family, which he interprets to mean that they were unpopular with the Presbytery. This would certainly have been the case in his father's time, and things in rural Scotland were slow to change. There is no direct evidence of John II's attitude to church matters, but the family tradition, of course, was Episcopalian, and this rather than covert Jacobitism may be why none of the four Johns held any public position. They were very much private people. The picture of John II given by this book could support the idea of him as a sort of factor of his own land, but we have seen that he was also a man of wider affairs.

John II knew the correspondence between his father and Governor Spotswood, for John I kept the drafts of his own letters as well as the

Governor's. After the latter's death John II exchanged accounts of the family with his executor in Virginia, the Revd. Robert Rose. As to the earlier history, John relied very much on the account written by his father as preface to an edition of Sir Robert's *Practicks*, but he also gives the fullest account of himself we are ever likely to have. The words cited above are from the longest of these documents, written from Spottiswoode on February 12th, 1745.

One other important facet of John II must be mentioned, his interest in monastic or other antiquities. There is evidence that in his later years he devoted much time to collecting information about former monastic houses in Scotland. The Earl of Buchan in 1786 described him as a diligent antiquary. There is not much material in the family papers, probably because after his death his son gathered it together and sent it to one of the experts of the time for evaluation. There are however several letters of the 1780s from a Lieutenant Hutton, written first from Barbados but later from Kelso, which seem to be part of a much larger correspondence about these antiquities. George Henry Hutton (d.1827) was the only son of Charles Hutton (1737–1823) the mathematician. He was a 2nd lieutenant in the Artillery in 1777, distinguished himself on active service in the West Indies, held commands in Ireland and was a Lt. General in 1821. He was deeply interested in Scottish antiquities, and made collections of antiquarian drawings and ecclesiastical documents, with a view to publishing a book.

In short, his interest was very much the same as John Spottiswoode's. As we see in both men, the active life was by no means incompatible with scholarship in that age. I do not know how John II came into contact with Hutton, how far their collaboration went, or when John first became closely involved with these subjects. John's name was traditionally quoted as the compiler of an account of former monastic houses in Scotland. As early as 1755 there was published in Edinburgh *A Large New Catalogue of the Bishops of the Several Sees within the Kingdom of Scotland down to the Year 1688*. To this was attached 'An Account of all the Religious Houses that were in Scotland at the Time of the Reformation' with a note 'NB This Work was compiled by the learned and ingenious Gentleman

John Spottiswood of Spottiswood, Esquire, the lineal representative of
the Most Reverend Father in GOD, John Spottiswood, Archbishop of St.
Andrews, and Lord High Chancellor of Scotland'. This was obviously a
highly sectarian publication, and seems to throw a different light on John
II's profile and activities. But was it really John II and not John I who
was being acknowledged? Although the blurb, as we might now call it,
does not say 'the late' John Spottiswood, or mention the profession of
advocate, it smacks much more of the father than of the son, and the son
was then only about 40 years of age. Unfortunately the family papers do
not clear up the confusion. Apart from the letters from Hutton and two
draft title pages which seem to show an intention to publish a work of
his own, the surviving papers consist of notes or amendments to an earlier
compilation.

What seems to have happened is that John III, perhaps not knowing
about Hutton's parallel work, took away his father's manuscripts and
showed them to the Earl of Buchan, who suggested the name of one
Mansfield Macdonald as a kind of editor. But apparently, even when his
father was still alive, John III was offering to sell them, in three volumes.[1]
It is not worth pursuing this minor obscurity among so many others. It
seems that the habit of pillaging the Spottiswoode papers has a long
history. All we can be sure of is that the subject of Scottish antiquities
remained close to John's heart, and must have been an important aspect
of his character. Eventually his work (or his father's) saw the light in a
more widely known publication of the nineteenth century, *Monasticon
Scoticon*.

In view of all that has been said, it may seem odd that John II allowed

---

1 See *Monasticon*, published by John Tweed, Glasgow 1868. This account of the
pre-Reformation buildings in Scotland is said to be 'based on Spottiswoode's'. On
the verso of the title page is a passage from a letter said to be addressed to General
Hutton by one J. Scotland on 8 June 1790: 'I am certainly informed that Mr
Spottiswood, of Spottiswood, in the neighbourhood of Kelso, has in MS the fullest
account of all the Religious Houses in Scotland, their lands and Revenues, that is
anywhere to be found; and that his son, Mr John Spottiswood, Solicitor of Law in
London, has been offering the MS, 3 vols, folio, to sale'.

his father's books to be put up for sale. Perhaps they represented to him an old-fashioned pedantry he wanted to be rid of. At any rate we find him writing down (a habit he inherited from the same pedantic father) his resolve to get rid of the remaining books of his father's and start a library of his own (NLS MS 10285): 'being resolved to purge my library of all of . . . yt left at . . . auction of my father's books and to make a small handsome collection of Classicks Civil Law and all of Scots Law together with some choice Books upon Gardenry and Husbandry &c.'. At the same time, 16th April 1735, he started an inventory of 'my books at Spottiswood', though whether this was before or after the 'purging' is not stated. There were just ten 'choice Books upon Gardenry and Husbandry', including one on falconry published in 1614. In all, 209 volumes were listed.

So already in 1735 John II was fully in possession of Spottiswoode and his interests were well-defined. Nearly 60 years later, in 1793, presumably soon after his death, another inventory of the library was made, showing that it had grown to nearly a thousand books. This time it was arranged according to location in the room. There were five presses, or in English bookcases, lettered A to E, each containing folio, quarto and 'octavo et infra' volumes. Of books outside the library, 'in the House', there were merely two – a Bible which had belonged to Archbishop Spottiswoode, and Anderson's *Diplomata Scotica*. John II's house guests evidently had to provide their own bedside reading!

7

The Unacknowledged
Improver

Tom barry's commentary tells us all we need to know about the detailed conduct of the work on the Spottiswoode estate over a period of 40 years. It was a period when Scotland, after a last convulsion in 1745, succumbed to a draconian *Pax Britannica* and began a slow climb to prosperity as part of a modern economic expansionist state. Those Scots who had resources of whatever kind were not slow to take advantage. Certainly the Spottiswoodes did – but the economic history of the family has yet to be written. Such a history would no doubt be able to trace an increasing involvement in all sorts of revenue-producing activities, such as road-building, toll-farming, lime production, mining, whaling, shipping, as well as the acquisition of government stocks and of more land by purchase or marriage; and of course the proceeds of lucrative legal practice. At present the evidence for these business ventures is mainly hearsay. John II was also familiar with the world of books, by which his father had profited, but it was his son who married the daughter of a great literary entrepreneur, and their descendants made the name of Spottiswoode famous all over the English-speaking world.

John II's financial resources, at the outset of his lairdship, are hard to gauge. He must have had some outside the estate, which was probably never a very lucrative one. At one point he received a large payment of back interest from the bank. If he was indeed receiving all the revenues of New Abbey, it is rather surprising that he did not cut more of a dash. Whatever his situation, he had enough to live in a style well above the average for a laird, and to begin the improvement of Spottiswoode. How much he originated, and how much he continued the work of his father, is open to question. Agricultural improvement had been in the air since John I's time. The 'Honourable Society of Improvers in the Knowledge of Agriculture in Scotland' was founded in 1723, with 300 members. Although John I cultivated a garden, he does not seem to have been an agriculturalist, while Tom Barry has made out a case for including John II among the better-known improvers such as Clerk of Penicuik or Cockburn of Ormiston. Some of these ruined themselves in the process, but John was more cautious.

In this Introduction the aim is to give only a general picture of John II as a man and his changes to the face of Spottiswoode. The ledger gives some important clues. John was not purely what might now be called a 'practical farmer'. He was also interested in the embellishment of the estate. One of the most intriguing entries in the ledger concerns his orders for sculpture from a mason, William Aitchison. Aitchison was paid for, among more workaday objects, statues of Jupiter, Juno and Venus (p.14, 11 November 1755) as well as for 'vases'. In 1759 he made 'statues of the 4 Seasons at 30 sh.ster. pr piece' which took him three days to set up at 14 pence a day. Years later he was still at it, supplying '1 Black Bearing a dial on his head Set up at the Mason's lodge', presumably a sundial (p.67, 6 November 1772). If these figures had survived they would be among the earliest sculptures attributable to a named country carver, at a time when the evidence of carved headstones suggests that a very primitive level of skill was the rule. There were not many outside pieces in the dispersal sale of Spottiswoode in 1935. It seems that what remained was disposed of piecemeal by the estate manager just before the demolition. A pair of eagles and some urns were taken to houses in the district, but they were probably of John III or John IV date.

Among the traditions in the family is one that John II bought extensively from Chippendale. There is no independent evidence of this yet, and if there was any documented Chippendale furniture in the dispersal sale, the auctioneers missed a trick. There is a story that Lady John Scott shipped some out to some of the estate cottages, as it had gone out of fashion. Had there been any left in 1935, it would doubtless have been sent to London for sale. John was certainly aware of Chippendale's innovations, for we find references to a 'Chinese rail' in 1768 and 1772. This would have been a fence, probably a low one surmounting a stone wall, made on the Chinese lattice or broken diagonal grid pattern used by Chippendale in his chairs in the Chinese taste. There are two surviving candidates for the 'sweep' where the Chinese rail was installed, assuming it was a low curved stone wall on the western approach to the house. But at both places the lattice has been replaced, if that is where it was, and probably more than once, by a low fence of more conventional design, which in its turn has rotted away amid local unconcern. Another of John II's flights of fancy which modern indifference put paid to, was his whalebone arches. An unnumbered sheet in the ledger, written in the first person, records the setting up of two pairs in the winter of 1767/68. One was on the main road into the estate a little way past the surviving stone arch, between the Pyatshaw school and schoolhouse. This pair survived into living memory. The record of inscriptions already referred to shows that the Pyatshaw whalebones stood on substantial stone piers bearing inscriptions in the same way as the present archway, whose effect it must have echoed. It is another reason for thinking the inscriptions were John II's work. And the mere existence of these bones strongly supports the putative whaling interest.

Generations of travellers on the high road from Edinburgh to the Border at Coldstream must have seen the archway on the north side of the road, without knowing that it leads into the Spottiswoode domain. This is not a conventional great house entrance with classical detailing and flanking lodges. An entrance of that kind is found two miles further along the high road. Embowered in trees, the Spottiswoode archway is 'gothick', with a pointed form of arch and two pinnacles on each side, all formed out of mortared rubble stonework. It has a primitive rusticity quite unlike the growing classicism of the eighteenth century. This seems as consistent with the character of John II as are the inscriptions set into its piers. It is tantalising that there is no reference in the ledger to the building of this archway or its companion on the far side of the estate, but their resemblance to the whalebone arches may make the 1760s their most probable date. On the other hand, there is an oral tradition connecting them to the battle of Blenheim (1704), in which case they would have been among the first improvements made to the estate by John I. The tradition may have arisen because John I's cousin, Alexander, was wounded at that battle. But their style is difficult to reconcile with this earlier date. Indeed their shape may suggest to some trained eyes a date considerably later than the 1760s. Although John II is the most likely author of the verses, there is always the possibility that the stones bearing them were repositioned in their present places at a later date, possibly at the time the record of them was made, that is referred to in the previous chapter.

As well as these embellishments, John II made more solid improvements to the fabric. He paid for slating the house (presumably replacing John I's pantiles) in 1771. But the very first page of the ledger, dated 1752, shows him fitting out an extension in the shape of two 'pavilions'. This is a common term for the symmetrical wings flanking the central block of a classical house, either attached to it directly, or linked by a corridor or colonnade. An example was Pencaitland House, where the pavilions survive while the main house has gone. It would have been perfectly natural for John II, who fathered a large family, to enlarge in this way the house John I had built.

However, a drainage plan of the estate, drawn up before the improvements under John IV, shows these pavilions at a considerable distance from the front corners of the house. There are other examples in Scotland of pavilions forming part of a symmetrical garden layout, rather than an adjunct to the house. At one end of the scale they would be called gazebos, but at the other they could be big enough to contain sizeable rooms on two floors. The pavilions at Spottiswoode were evidently of this kind, but they were not joined to the house even by a parterre, but stood far apart at the entrance to a large rectangular garden.

Aside from this drainage plan, there is some evidence for the existence of a formal garden at Spottiswoode, or at least the intention to have one. As already mentioned, there are three somewhat rudimentary layouts for a simple formal design, inscribed Spottiswoode, one of which includes the little elevation of the presumed house of John I. They are in the possession of Dr. W.A. Brogden of the Scott Sutherland School of Architecture at Aberdeen. Dr. Brogden considers them to be by an amateur, and probably of the early eighteenth century. Apart from the drawing of the house they are not informative, for they are vague about the relationship between the house and the garden, and tell us nothing about the scale of the project. But they have an interesting provenance, having come from the dispersal sale of Saltoun Castle in East Lothian, the home of Andrew Fletcher (1655–1716), the opponent of Union with England. In his later years Fletcher was a pioneering improver, and it is not impossible that the Spottiswoode drawings were the result of discussion between him and John I on how the latter might improve his surroundings.

But to return to the pavilions, one at least of them was being fitted out as a library in 1752, for we read of '3 glass doors for the book presses in the easter pavilion', but the west pavilion also had presses, purpose undefined. The pavilions also seem to have had more domestic uses, for one entry refers to lining (i.e. panelling) 'above the alcove bed', and another to a nursery and 'Doctor's Room' in the upper storey. The same wright, Robert Mason, must have been doing work in the main house as well, providing three press doors in 'the old library room'. All this work suggests at least that by 1752 John II had settled on Spottiswoode as his main residence.

The most intriguing scrap of evidence concerning John II's activities at Spottiswoode is not in the ledger but in a small sheet among the family papers (NLS MS 10285, f. 115) in which John claims to have found traces of a Roman wall running from above Blythe to Paxton by way of Greenlaw. He quotes a man named Nisbet 'who drove timber to me from Berwick about the year 1753 when I built the *Tomb* to the house of Spottiswoode' (my italics, and I cannot read the word as anything but 'tomb'). Whatever was this, and why did a tomb, which one would expect to be made of stone, need considerable quantities of timber? There is no other reference to such a thing. But hidden among the entries about the pavilions are three concerning a grotto, which had windows and a glazed door. Could this conceivably have had a hidden purpose as a memorial to John's ancestors? Needless to say, among the general destruction, no trace of any of this has survived.

With these intriguing glimpses of the architectural development of Spottiswoode, the question must arise whether John II or his father was acting alone or with architectural advice. I have found nothing to associate Spottiswoode with a named architect until the time of John IV. The very little evidence we have about John I's house suggests that it was a simple building in the vernacular, which at that date meant symmetry but few other concessions to classicism. But the existence of garden plans, however tentative and rudimentary, and the use of pavilions, show that a designing hand was at work during the first half of the eighteenth century, even if the hand was that of a gentleman amateur rather than a professional. That said, the contribution of gentlemen amateurs at that period was of the greatest importance.

The most prominent architect in Scotland during the period, say 1710 to 1740, was William Adam. Adam's practice was a good deal among the up-and-coming gentry rather than the established grandees, and he himself had the same entrepreneurial disposition as the Spottiswoodes. Moreover, in that age when personal knowledge and kinship meant so much, Adam worked for two Lothian and Border families who were connected by marriage to the Spottiswoodes, the Bairds at Newbyth and the Wauchopes at Broomlands, near Kelso. He may also have worked for John II's parents-in-law the Thomsons, who in the decade following his marriage built a large and handsome house of the Adam type on their estate of Charleton in East Fife. The house still stands, though with many later additions and alterations. It is very unlikely that William Adam ever produced a full-dress design for a house at Spottiswoode, or some trace of it would have survived. It would not be worth even mentioning him in this connection, but for a little bit of architectural evidence.

The only part of John II's building operations, apart from the arches, to have survived is the 'offices'. These consist of a symmetrical rectangular courtyard open to the south, the long side centred on a substantial house for the head groom or coachman, flanked by open sheds (shades) supported by Doric columns, which sheds are now filled in and partly incorporated in the house. The two short sides contain stables and coach-houses. The gable ends of these sides have loading doors at the upper level, in the form of Gothic lancets, and on the lower level two circular blind windows apiece. In the centre of the first floor of the house is a Palladian window with heavily Baroque detailing, which corresponds in every respect to the type employed by William Adam on many occasions. Even more remarkable, the blind circular windows have triple blocked keystones at the north, south, east and west positions. This was a detail used by Adam at Chatelherault, the Duke of Hamilton's 'dog-kennel' and banqueting house of 1732 (though here with single blocked keystones) but as far as I can see nowhere else. The problem is that the ledger suggests that these buildings were not erected until the 1770s, thirty years after William Adam's death. Was there some sketch lying about that John II could have handed to his masons? Or could the building have been begun, and then left uncompleted until the later date? Admittedly William Adam's style formed the basis of the mid-eighteenth century vernacular in Scotland, but this fidelity to a detail seems unusual.

We have seen that John II was an antiquarian, and not only in his old age. His concern with a 'tomb to the house of Spottiswoode' as early as 1753 is more evidence in the same direction. In John's time there would still have been evidence above ground of the antiquity of the place. Nobody knows when the old tower was pulled down, or where it stood. Tom Barry suggests that it may have been elsewhere on the estate. But when Sir Robert Douglas was collecting information for his *Baronage of Scotland*, John II must have given his place of residence as 'the old castle at Spottiswoode', for so Douglas has it. Since he had made all these improvements to his father's house, he presumably lived in it. So what did he mean? Did he use the old tower as a sort of retreat? Or was 'the old castle at Spottiswoode' a rhetorical way of expressing his devotion to the past? It would have been a frame of mind suitable to the 'primitive character' that John I had boasted that the family maintained.

The other ancient building that stood on the site was the mediaeval chapel, which, John I wrote, was called 'The White Chapel, the Vestige of which is still remaining' (in his preface to Sir Robert Spottiswoode's *Practicks*). According to the Statistical Account of the Parish of West-ruther, published in 1845, the vestige was removed to make way for the 'offices', which have already been described. Fortunately for Spottis-woode, these offices survived the wholesale demolition of 1938. We can be pretty sure that they are the same as the offices which Thomas Grieve was paid for building in May 1777. There is a doorway in the corner of the office yard with the date 1796, and this has been taken as the date of the whole. But the style of the building is impossible to reconcile with this date; it is old-fashioned even for 1777. Moreover, on the west wing of the stables there is another datestone very clearly incised 1770. It is high up over a fairly recent large sliding door probably put in by John Herbert-Spottiswoode. Either it was simply raised from its position above the original door there, or it comes from elsewhere in the buildings. As to the doorway dated 1796, it must have been inserted during the im-provements of the last years of the century mentioned below, under the management of John III or his aunt Rachael Bedlay. The evidence of datestones can thus be confusing, but it seems that work on the 'offices' went on for a long time before and after we find Grieve working there in 1777. Two years later Robert Birnie was paid for roofing 'the east shades (and) stables'. As already noted, these buildings have details remi-niscent of the work of William Adam half a century before. The one inconsistent feature is the Gothic windows, and even odder, the circular blind windows underneath them, one of the William Adam-like details already referred to, have painted tracery in imitation of Gothic rose windows. John II would have known the 'gothick' chapel at Yester, dating from the 1750s, which incorporated a blind pointed arch and an oculus on the west front (AHSS [Architectural Heritage Society of Scotland] Journal, iv, 1993, N.M. Cameron). Knowing John's antiquarian interests, and reflecting that he may have pulled down the ruins of the chapel in order to build these offices, this could perhaps have been his way of perpetuating its presence.

How much of what John II made can still be seen? His house, pavilions, his grotto, whalebone arches, statuary, have all gone. The 'offices' survive, as do the stone archways already described. Thousands of travellers on the A697 must also have noticed the so-called Clock Lodges on the long straight six miles west of Greenlaw, more properly known as the Eagle Lodge, from the eagles which formerly stood on the gate piers. This became the formal entrance to Spottiswoode. It consists of a pair of Georgian lodge houses, flanking a pillared entrance gate. It is a conventional enough entrance to a prosperous eighteenth-century estate, save for one feature. Terminating each lodge on the side away from the gates is a flat chimneystack like a toy tower with chimneys for battlements. On them are prominent clock faces on which the painted hands stand forever at the times, so tradition has it, of the passing stage coaches. On the front of each lodge are also panels giving the distances to various towns to north and south. The most obvious reference here is to the new ease of transport along new roads surfaced by Macadam, a development that was taking place towards the end of John II's lifetime. The eccentricity of the whole group is typical of him, but he was by no means the only eccentric in the family. In his old age, and after his death in 1793, the management of the estate was carried on by his daughter Rachael, to whose time belongs the charming but ruinous classical dog-kennel adjacent to the 'offices', which bears the date 1798. The Eagle Lodges were referred to as recently built in the *Kelso Chronicle* in 1801, but it is possible that the clocks and panels were added later under John IV, whose wealth would have lent even more conviction to the idea of Spottiswoode as a centre of activity and important stage for posts and travellers.

John II's work on improving the land can be studied in Tom Barry's commentary on the ledger. Here we need only note how John's planting relates to what can be seen on the ground today. There is frequent reference in the ledger to men working in the 'strips'. This is a puzzling word to anyone familiar with the curvaceous outlines of the present fields and woods. In fact, the original plan for the enclosure or afforestation of the estate was severely rectangular. The first evidence of it comes from Roy's military map of Scotland after the '45, surveyed between 1752 and 1755. This shows the house in the centre of an almost complete square, divided into four sections by radiating avenues. It is not clear whether the enclosure lines are trees, or merely hedges. The pattern suggests agricultural enclosure rather than a formal landscape garden layout, such as jumps out of Roy's map at Mellerstain nearby. But Roy does enclose it by a red line, a convention he uses for indicating pleasure grounds.

There is no evidence whether this plan was originally laid down by him or by John I, but it is certain that John II planted immense numbers of trees. He however seems to have worked to a somewhat different scheme, which we can see in a map of 1773. Taking the axis of the house (which faced slightly east of south) as a starting line, three belts of woodland (the strips) were planted running south-south-east until they met either the edge of the estate, or land too boggy to be planted. The view from the house and pavilions would thus have been bounded on each side by one of these strips of woodland. The neighbouring estate of Wedderlie still exhibits much the same pattern today; indeed with its original Laird's house, and a similar site, it must give quite a close approximation to the appearance of Spottiswoode at the end of the eighteenth century. In its aim to impose order on an undeveloped landscape, the arrangement was not too different from that shown by Roy, and may still reflect John I's intentions. It stops far short of the grandiose interventions in the landscape that often accompanied greater houses of the period, with their radiating walks, canals, obelisks and fountains. As just noted, there was a conspicuous example of this not far off in Roy's portrayal of Mellerstain. John II's fancy in this direction, as we have seen, was more modest, and suitable to the transitional period between the grandiose style of landscape gardening and the naturalism of Capability Brown.

In the absence of evidence that John II employed a known landscape gardener, he cannot be clearly placed in the history of the art. As we have seen, he had ideas, but they were probably inconsistent, sometimes old-fashioned, sometimes original. The undated, unsigned plans for the garden referred to above are very basic formal layouts for the area south of the house, which could have been drawn up by anybody at any time during the first forty years or so of the century. The space may have been intended to be filled with different forms of planting, as William Adam specified for the parterre of Arniston House in 1726 (Tait: *The Landscape Garden in Scotland*, Edinburgh 1980, p.28). Although it had a wide view, the site at Spottiswoode had no natural features close at hand. For his closer prospects John II was dependent on tree-planting. Blackadder's map of 1797 shows his park divided into long enclosures by the strips already mentioned, and the one facing the house terminated by another strip at right angles. How the grotto or 'tomb' fitted into this scheme cannot be known. Such features were not uncommon: for example Sir John Clerk had a grotto at Penicuik in the 1730s. It seems that John II did not push the ideas of any one school of landscape very far.

The first Ordnance Survey map of Spottiswoode, surveyed in 1856, still shows the traces of John II's strips, overlaid by the far more elaborate planting of his grandson. No more than a slight vestige can be seen today. But the curving lines of the road from the Coldstream highway to Spottiswoode, lined by strips of woodland, survive from John II's time.

8

The London Connection

JOHN SPOTTISWOODE died in 1793 at the great age of 81 or 82. He had sired eight children, six of whom survived him. His settlement was rather eccentric, as befitted the man, but not to the extent of defying primogeniture. So the eldest son, John III, got the estate but his fourth child and eldest daughter, Rachael, got the livestock and implements 'which shall be upon the parks around the house and upon the farm or ground in my natural possession'. She also got the chaise, harness and chaise horses. This Rachael had married a laird, Archibald Roberton of Bedlay in Lanarkshire, but they had no children and Rachael seems to have spent much time at Spottiswoode and to have become her father's manager in his old age. John II's will spells out that her husband is excluded from *jus mariti* over his wife's bequest, which is not to be attachable for his debts. He goes on to make very unequal bequests to his second and third sons and to three of his granddaughters, including one who, from the wording of the bequest, may have been illegitimate.

Since John III was by then a man of 52 with an established legal practice in London, he presumably had no thought of taking up permanent residence as a Laird in Scotland. So it was a good thing for the estate that one of the daughters was able and willing to take on its management. Of the other two sons, one had taken himself off to the West Indies, dying in Tobago in the same year as his father. The other, if we may judge by the very small legacy left him, was not in favour with his father. Under Rachael's management Spottiswoode continued to develop. The charming little dog kennel with a pedimented facade in whin and sandstone bears the Spottiswoode eagle and the date 1798. It survived the demolition of 1938 but has become ruinous since. Rachael Bedlay lived until 1817, while her brother John III died in 1805. His heir, John IV, was then 25, and as a young man-about-London was probably glad to leave the day-to-day conduct of Spottiswoode to his aunt, although as we shall see, he played his part in local affairs.

In reality there is no knowing how far Rachael's influence went, for the papers give no clue to the family politics and customs of the time. After John II's death in 1793 no Laird resided permanently for at least forty years. That did not necessarily mean that the house and grounds were neglected, or greatly underused. In August 1795 it was the location of a business meeting between an author, Thomas Somerville, and his prospective publishers, the firm founded by John III's father-in-law (*Life and Times of Thomas Somerville (1711–1814)*, Edinburgh 1861, p.291). This may not have been a rare event, and the time of year fits the seasonal pattern we would expect from men of affairs with estates in Scotland. The same half-century saw a transformation of the British, and particularly the Scottish, economy, which brought radical changes to the upper levels of society. Greater wealth, and the growth of the money supply, joined with improved transport to give John II's son, and even more his grandson, a freedom of movement he himself never enjoyed. It became ever easier for Scottish landowners to spend time in London, and for Scotsmen in London, or Englishmen, to travel to Scotland to shoot, fish and climb. For this was the beginning of the 'discovery', or some would say the exploitation, of Scotland by the wealthy classes of Europe. Johns III and IV, with their existing interests in London, fit neatly into this pattern. Perhaps it was not after all Rachael's idea to build a dog kennel. Her brother may have been accustomed to have shooting parties and so need more room for gundogs, or he may have decided to keep a pack of hounds. On the other hand agricultural buildings were also put up during the non-resident period. The mill buildings bear a datestone of 1796, the little home farm steading has one of 1825, with the initials of John IV.

The period c.1798 to 1805 seems to have been prosperous and exciting for Spottiswoode. New roads were being laid out, and the new coaching inn at Whiteburn, which still exists as a private house, was inaugurated in October 1800 with a grand dinner, to serve travellers on them. The long avenue to the Eagle or 'clock' lodge linked Spottiswoode House with a convenient stretch of the high road and was a stopping-place for coaches. The troop of yeomanry cavalry was established, which is more fully described in the next chapter. Not least, as an indication of improved agriculture, Spottiswoode bred a famously gigantic ox, which was painted by Alexander Nasmyth and engraved by Ward and by J. Berryman (the original by Nasmyth is in the Royal Museum of Scotland). It is impossible to say how much John III, or his son John IV, or his sister Rachael, were individually responsible for so much activity. One can only speculate that the youthful energies of the future Laird had a good deal to do with it.

John Spottiswoode III was born in 1741. In this narrative he would be a shadowy figure, for there are few clues to his character, but for the testimony of James Boswell. It seems that John III, as a Scots solicitor in London, working probably mainly for Scottish clients, was in the habit of putting work in the penurious Boswell's way. Between 1772 and 1778 there are many references to 'Mr Spottiswoode the solicitor', instructing him in various cases. Boswell does not offer us the trenchant description he gives of John II, but one entry shows that John III may have inherited something of the 'drollery', or as we might now put it, facetiousness, of his father. Boswell (10 April 1772) describes supping with John III and his wife ('a good-looking woman') at their house with 'a kind of company of Jews and Portuguese'. Boswell huffily remarks that he was 'surprised and plagued with a kind of punning and playing upon words with which he [Spottiswoode] persisted to entertain us all the evening, instead of being the sensible man of business that I had been accustomed to see him'.

Boswell might be used to being a butt of Dr Johnson, but it was evidently a bit thick to be put on the spot by a fellow Scot, and he was as surprised as we are today to discover the cosmopolitan company that John III kept. This was not confined to 'Jews and Portuguese'. About 1777 John III was one of a company which included Johnson, Sir Joshua Reynolds, Bennet Langton the Greek scholar and the Marchese Gherardi, as well as Boswell, at the house of General Paoli the hero of Corsican independence. Boswell casts Spottiswoode as the principal feeder of lines to service Johnson's *bon mots*, though giving him none of his own. But elsewhere he provides our only direct report of John III's opinions, when Boswell makes him say: 'I love a large society, where men do not come close so as to be rubbed, but are packed with a deal of interjacent circumstances, as hay or wool, to keep them safe'. At this date when the New Town was just beginning to take shape, and the Scottish nobility and gentry still had their town houses in the crowded closes of the Old, Edinburgh society would evidently not have answered to this description. We can see here the beginning of the transformation of the Spottiswoodes from their 'primitive' Scottishness to membership of the British ascendancy.

So John III was the link between the pawky laird mocked by Boswell and that young man of the Regency, grown Victorian gentleman, John IV. Here the 'good-looking woman', John III's wife, comes into focus. Margaret Strahan was more than a good-looking woman, she was a considerable heiress. Not, however, heiress to old money. Her father, William Strahan, was born in Edinburgh in 1715, the son of an exciseman, and at the age of 22 was a Freeman of the Stationers Company in London. He married in 1738 the daughter of an Episcopalian clergyman of Edinburgh, at that time an uncomfortable profession and a possible early link with the Spottiswoodes. With a partner named Millar he set up a printing business which became the most successful in London, at a time when the printing and publishing businesses were closely linked or identical. The firm printed Johnson's Dictionary in 1755. Strahan became a friend of Johnson and many other intellectuals of the time, Adam Smith, David Home, Edward Gibbon among them. As we have seen, his son-in-law John III also became familiar with this circle. In 1766 Strahan acquired a third share in the patent of King's Printer from the holder, Charles Eyre. (Eyre was of an English family and has no apparent connection with the Eyre of Canonmills in Edinburgh who had married John III's sister.) In 1774 Strahan was rich enough to support the expense of being elected to Parliament as Member for Malmesbury in Wiltshire. On his death in 1785 he left a fortune of about £100,000 – a huge sum at that date (R.A. Austen-Leigh: *The Story of a Printing-House*, privately printed, 1912).

William Strahan's only daughter Margaret Penelope married John III in 1779. Their first son, John IV, was born the following year. Two of their younger sons, Andrew and Robert, succeeded their uncle Andrew Strahan as partners in the printing business, and thus began the firm of Eyre and Spottiswoode whose name, as the imprint on Bibles and prayer books, became known throughout the English-speaking world. This also signals the divergence between the two branches of the family. While the eldest son was destined for the Scottish estate, his brothers' interests were now entirely in London and they had the means to establish themselves as landed proprietors in the south. Andrew built a country house, Broomhall, in Surrey, but while in London lived at Carlton House Terrace, than which there could hardly be a grander address, much grander than his elder brother's town house in Great George Street. We must assume that, as he grew up, John IV moved in an atmosphere of considerable elegance and sophistication.

The English branch of the family cannot be part of this narrative, although they may have preserved many traditions, or even records, of their Scottish forebears. Besides Andrew and Robert, John had two brothers who were apprenticed to the printing business. One, William, died as a youth. The other, George, did not continue in the business but became a Lieutenant-Colonel in the Army. He returned to Scotland and lived at Gladswood, a handsome house in a wonderful position on the Tweed near Dryburgh. Of his four sisters, one died in infancy and two more married and had children. The other, Mary, was a rebel who defied all the taboos of that pious family and censorious age, and outdoing her Aunt Macfarlane Spottiswoode, bore two children out of wedlock to two fathers.

The New Statistical Account of the Parish of Westruther was published in 1845 but written in 1834. Like all the other parish accounts it was the work of the minister, the Revd. Robert Jamieson, and is an extensive study of every aspect of the place, its topography, natural features, land ownership and above all its agriculture. The minister looked back, from his position on the threshold of modernity, to a time within living memory when (quoting a trivial indicator) there were only three teakettles in the parish, and when the population of the little settlement among the marshes was entirely cut off from the outside world. In a few generations more the encyclopaedic knowledge he laid claim to would have seemed ridiculous in a clergyman. It was a perfect opportunity to record profound change, which Mr Jamieson seized with both hands, and his 25-page essay is readable throughout. As the largest estate and the oldest family of the place, mention of Spottiswoode often recurs. The traditions Jamieson relied on had long roots; they were not the products of a romantic attachment to the picturesque, as they might have been later in the century. Thus his account of there being a chapel at Spottiswoode of the period of David II (1329–71) can be believed, and indeed he says that the baptismal font has been preserved. However, the old font in the present kirk at Westruther is reported to have come from Bassendean, not Spottiswoode.

This is perhaps a digression, but as we have seen, the landowning class was also in a state of transition, and it is interesting to read what Jamieson says about them. The preceding Old Statistical Account, published in 1799, was terse and short and made no mention of the Spottiswoodes whatever. Jamieson however gave a potted history of the family, and is evidently even-handed about their episcopalianism. Naming six families who own land in the parish, he writes: 'Of these families, the Laird of Spottiswoode is the only large proprietor, and the only one who resides, though he too has hitherto been an absentee during one half of the year'. Jamieson was writing at the very time when John IV was building his grand new house: 'The only modern mansion is the new house now in the course of being built at Spottiswoode. It is in the old English style . . . The new house is connected with the old family mansion, which has undergone very important alterations, so that the whole will have a unique appearance. It is not yet completed, but was fitted up in a temporary, but elegant style, on a late auspicious occasion, the marriage of Mr Spottiswoode's second daughter to Sir Hugh Campbell of Marchmont, MP for Berwickshire'.

The mid-1830s was therefore a climactic time for Spottiswoode, when the estate was once again to have a resident proprietor. John IV was in his mid-50s, his children were growing up, and a more settled life may well have appealed to him. We only have Mr Jamieson's word that he had been absent half the year, and his family may have spent much more time in Scotland. Certainly his daughter Alicia Anne grew up to love Scotland and cordially hate London. Whatever the circumstances, since the death of John II the family had accumulated considerable wealth, in ways that still remain largely hearsay. Without the evidence we do not have to believe the tradition that the family developed a pigeon post, and were thus able to get prior knowledge of national events affecting the market. There were plenty of more credible sources, as well as the law and the publishing industry. They evidently made John IV a rich man, and when he returned permanently to Scotland he determined to live there in style. It was a great period of house-building in Scotland, as castle keeps and even the neat classical rectangles of the eighteenth century were everywhere found inadequate for the burgeoning families and new-fangled luxuries of the mid-nineteenth century. At least John IV did not destroy the earlier house as many owners did, but only made 'very important alterations' to it. Whether he was guilty of clearing away the original tower house remains unknown. For his new house John IV chose a Scottish architect with one of the largest country-house practices in Britain, William Burn.

9

The High Victorians

BEFORE WE TURN to the changes John IV made to the estate, what
sort of picture can we form of him? The archives contain little of a
personal kind. But a sympathetic picture is drawn by Helen Warrender,
granddaughter of the daughter who married Sir Hugh Campbell in 1834.
In 1911 Helen Warrender wrote the only biographical study that exists
of Alicia Anne, Lady John Scott, John IV's eldest child, as an introduction
to an edition of Alicia's songs and verses. Though she naturally has more
to say of Alicia's husband than of her father, her portrait of the latter is
of a solid, reassuring presence. 'The Laird was a very remarkable man.
He had been bred to the law and before his marriage had travelled much.
To a calm, well-balanced mind he added great exercise of common sense.
His own property was admirably managed and through the whole of his
long life his advice was constantly sought by others.' He was, she wrote,
'a big, fine commanding-looking man', and it was from him that Alicia
inherited her love of botany, geology and especially archaeology. He also
ensured that Alicia and her sister were well educated, which was not
always the case in the gentry class at that period, or since. The surviving
correspondence of John IV, scattered through various manuscript collections in the National Library, bears out the picture of a benign, pragmatic,
early Victorian gentleman, even though it mainly consists of short business
or social notes. We can be pretty sure that in John IV there remained
nothing of the 'braid-Scots man' of John II, or of the facetious manner
of John III. The well-known Spottiswoode eccentricity is more evident
in his daughter Alicia. In his time, the connections of the Spottiswoodes,

already wide in Scotland, spread outwards until they became finished members of the British upper class.

Upper class, but not, strictly speaking, governing class. After the ill-fated Lord President Robert Spottiswoode, and the Governor of Virginia, no member of the family held public office. At first this must certainly have been due to their association with the lost cause and their continuing Episcopalianism. Such prejudice may well have lasted into the nineteenth century. The British ascendancy had ways of smoothing out these difficulties for its successful members, and but for the collapse of the family succession after John IV's death, all avenues of advancement would have been open to them. A key question, however, in John IV's lifetime, was still religion. There is no firm evidence about how the later Spottiswoodes conducted themselves in religious affairs when at home in Scotland. John II and his wife were buried (or possibly re-buried) in the old kirk at Westruther, the earliest of the family to have a visible tomb there; and a very plain tombstone it is. Yet, as noted, the minister of the time ignored them in his account of the Parish. On the other hand, the gravestones of John IV and his daughter, as well as of the other family of those generations who are buried there, bear Christian affirmations that no minister of the kirk would have found wanting in faith. John IV was in correspondence with Principal Lee of Edinburgh University, a theologian who was instrumental in trying to move the worship of the kirk away from its early primitivism into a more gracious form that permitted music and read prayers. It is a reasonable assumption that part of John IV's return to play the part of a large Scottish landowner was a sort of personal accommodation with the kirk, burying the antagonism that had lasted since the bloody events of two hundred years before.

In the absence of very much written evidence about the character and standing of John IV, the house he built is the most important statement he made. It has been demolished, but there are photographs of it in its Victorian prime, and a complete set of plans and elevations exists in the National Monuments Record of Scotland. William Burn (1787–1870) was in his forties when John IV commissioned him, but he had built or altered over fifty Scottish houses before Spottiswoode, and was to build many more before transferring his practice to London in 1844. Among his less spectacular works was one that John IV would probably have known well, a wing at his grandmother Thomson's family house at Charleton in Fife. But in fact, as this was built in 1833, John would have placed his commission already, for work was far enough advanced by the summer of 1834 to provide a temporary setting for his daughter's wedding, as we have seen. Whereas the existing house at Spottiswoode was smaller than Charleton, John IV's commission was much bigger. It was in fact for a whole new large house, which would have been sufficient in itself, without the retention of the earlier one. I have seen no photograph of Spottiswoode that includes the fronts of both houses. The visual relationship between them must have been a little odd even after Burn's attempt to harmonise them. It says a lot for John IV's family piety that he wanted to retain the old house, and it seems that members of the family continued to have rooms there right up to the time when it was finally abandoned.

William Burn's great success as a builder of country houses is remarkable considering that he not only bridged the divide between Scotland and England, but was equally successful in the very different atmospheres of late-Georgian and mid-Victorian Britain. He could not have been so without a great deal of flexibility, or what critics of the arts call eclecticism. To put it crudely, he was an architectural trimmer, who could easily turn from one 'style' to another. But an eclectic architect is more likely to give a client what he really wants than one with firm stylistic convictions. John IV's own life, too, had spanned the transition from the Regency to the age of Reform, and from a Scottish to a British class ascendancy. So it surely fitted his sense of identity to have Burn design a house that was neither neo-classical nor Scottish vernacular, which had been Burn's alternative styles before that date. Instead, he made use of his architect's most successful manner of the 1830s – the Jacobethan. Spottiswoode House was by no means the most graceful of Burn's buildings in this style, since John IV's desire for accommodation dictated a solid block on three floors. But it was well-planned, as all Burn's buildings were, and, with its more than twenty bedrooms, gave all the scope John IV could have wanted for the extensive house-parties that improved

communications were making so much more possible. The family tradition
has it that it had an early form of central heating by hot air passages,
which caused insurance companies wonderful alarm in later years. The
house proclaimed no Scottish allegiance, as some of Burn's later baronial
houses did. Those were the product of a pro-Scottish romanticism that
could be safely indulged, in the wake of Queen Victoria's Balmoral, by
Scots and English alike. That time had not yet arrived in the 1830s, when
it was still the object of the Scottish upper or middling classes to identify
themselves as closely as possible with their English equivalents. As we
shall see, John IV's daughter took a very different line.

If the house proclaimed no Scottish allegiance, it certainly proclaimed
the accumulated wealth of the Spottiswoode family. With its Gothic belfry
rising to over sixty-five feet in height, it was a huge feature of the lower
slopes of Lammermuir. Internally it combined grandeur of scale with a
feeling for domestic comfort and security that was to have a sequel in
thousands of rich mercantile houses in Victoria's reign. A study of the
plans reveals the ingenious fitting-in of domestic accommodation – bedrooms, dressing rooms, closets and cupboards – for which Burn was well
known. Such a house, with its ornamental gardens, required the services
of a battalion of servants, who could not possibly have been accommo-
dated in the old house. In the lonely depopulated countryside of west
Berwickshire today, it is difficult to imagine the existence of the equivalent
of a sizeable village centred on the great house alone. The benign elderly
Victorian Laird in his library, surrounded by an extended family of cousins
as depicted by Margaret Warrender, seems also a world away from his
grandfather John II, carefully entering the debt owed to him by one of
his labourers for half a braxy sheep.

In fact, things did not go altogether well for John IV and his family.
But before we consider the upshot, we should look at the other changes
John made to the appearance of the place. After the stable court, which
survives, the biggest ancillary building was the so-called Eagle Hall,
which does not. I have no certain evidence to show whether it was built
near the end of John III's time (he died in 1805) or in the early years of
John IV. Photographs would suggest a date well after 1810, but before

the classical vernacular of Scotland was superseded by the British 'national' style of Tudor-Jacobethan which clothed the house itself. Eagle Hall consisted of twin two-storey blocks (perhaps an echo of John II's pavilions?) joined by a single storey range of arched openings, with the flat-headed arches found also in the home farm steading of 1825. Surprisingly for such a practical and well-built structure, which would have made a charming house, it found no buyer in 1935 and went the same way as the mansion.

The story of Eagle Hall is intriguing. At the time of the sale, it served as the estate office, a laundry and joiner's shop. Before that, Lady John Scott, John IV's daughter, used to keep her collection of antiquities there. But earlier still, it seems to have been the headquarters of a troop of yeomanry cavalry, and this was probably its original purpose. A detailed account of the Borders regiments of yeomanry cavalry was published in the *Proceedings* of the Hawick Archaeological Society for 1915. The first two troops of the Berwickshire Yeomanry Cavalry were raised around Duns in 1797. Although they were not part of the regular army, they were granted a small allowance by the Government, and their commanders were given royal commissions. Four years later, in 1801, we read that Captain John Spottiswoode of Spottiswoode had raised a third troop. Although he was not yet Laird, it seems probable that this was John IV rather than his solicitor father, and it may be no coincidence that he came of age in that year.

In 1801, as in 1797, the main purpose of the Scottish, like the English, yeomanry cavalry was to repel invasion by the French, and when this risk receded they were meant to be stood down. But not before, quite accidentally, their state of readiness had been tested. In 1803 the system of warning beacons on strategic hilltops had been revived, something not seen in Scotland since the English harrying of the Border in the sixteenth century. In January 1804 the watchers at Hume Castle mistakenly thought they saw the southerly beacon fired, and lighted their own. Soon the whole Border was up in arms, and not only the cavalry. The Laird of Mellerstain is said to have ridden out in his carpet slippers, calling out his tenantry as he went. The whole Borders regiments, with other volunteers, had mustered at Dunbar before the mistake was generally known. Beside this, the regular exercises that took place at Duns and Berwick must have seemed tame, but they were certainly the excuse for much conviviality.

The Berwickshire troops wore green with red facings, although they were known as the Berwickshire Blues. In 1817 the title 'Eagle Troop' is first recorded as the name of the 3rd Troop, and this may be a clue to the date of the Eagle Hall. By this time the purpose of the cavalry had changed. The war was over, but the possibility of civil unrest (which had always existed), or even revolution, had never been higher. Although Spottiswoode was far from the industrial districts, the agricultural labourers in Berwickshire were numerous, and very poor. William Cobbett, touring Scotland in 1832, was unfavourably impressed by the factory-like conditions of the farm workers in Northumberland and over the Border. So in 1817 the numbers and training of the yeomanry cavalry were actually increased. In 1818 the strength of the Eagle Troop was 51 officers and men. In the event, all that they were called to do was to attend a riot between Irish sheep-shearers and the local people in Lauder in 1821, and keep order at a public hanging at Fans, near Gordon. In 1823 they took part in the great parade before King George IV on Portobello sands. In 1826 John IV was promoted second-in-command of the Regiment, and handed over command of the Eagle Troop to a Captain Thomas Bruce.

The Berwickshire Yeomanry Cavalry was disbanded in 1828 as a Government economy measure. The Commanding Officer, Lt. Col. Hay, told his men that 'the saving to the Government by this reduction was as paltry as the remuneration was to the Yeomanry, and he was quite sure it could have no weight with that Corps, and that they would be equally ready to serve without it'. They were allowed to keep their uniforms, but I am not sure about their arms. Obviously the sense of solidarity, the discipline and the social ritual involved would have been very important to an estate such as Spottiswoode, and would not willingly be discontinued. Something of a military tradition seems to have lingered on at Spottiswoode, where the isolated setting might well have encouraged a defensive state of mind.

The records of the Cavalry also throw some extra light on the young

John IV and his relationship to the estate. His role as Captain may not have been very time-consuming, but it does suggest he was at Spottiswoode more than one might expect of John III's son. Sometimes it is hard to know whether father or son is being referred to, as on the occasion when John Spottiswoode presided at a convivial dinner at the opening of the newly built Whiteburn Inn, after the completion of the road to Kelso. John IV can only have been twenty or twenty-one at the time.

We must return to the physical condition of Spottiswoode. As far as one can tell, John II died content with his planting at Spottiswoode, conceived on the rectangular model which can still be seen on the neighbouring estate of Wedderlie. Nothing is known of any planting carried out by John III in the seventeen years of his possession. But such a transformation as John IV wrought on the house of Spottiswoode entailed also a major transformation of the policies and parks surrounding the house. The loss of all the papers concerning this period of the estate's history means that we have no way of knowing what professional advisers John IV employed. We know that he employed William Burn only because Burn's own plans for the house have survived. So far no landscape architect or garden designer has been identified. The only clue is provided by Margaret Warrender, who informs us that John IV learned the method of moving full-grown trees from Sir Henry Steuart of Allanton in Lanarkshire, and used it to turn the meadow south of the gardens into a deer park on the English model, which came to be known as the Lawn Park. In fact Steuart passed the method on to many Scots landowners and improvers, including Sir Walter Scott, who was scathing about his intelligence (*Letters* vol 8, p.91). Warrender wanted us to think that her great-grandfather was responsible for everything good about Spottiswoode, which had been until then a barren waste. But she failed to account for the fact that the trees could have come only a short distance, in fact, almost certainly from the estate itself. Most likely, they were taken from those planted by John II in a now unfashionable pattern.

Sir Henry Steuart (1759–1836), a baronet, soldier and historian, had a great influence on landscape through his book *The Planter's Guide* published in 1828 (see A.A. Tait: *The Landscape Garden in Scotland 1735–1835*,

Edinburgh 1980). It may well be that he advised John IV on the planning
of his woods, as well as imparting the technique of 'jankering', as moving
big trees was called. Steuart's ideas on how to lay out fields and woods
nearest to the great house were not specially original. Park landscapes
similar to his own at Allanton were found all over the country at the
beginning of the nineteenth century. They were the antithesis of John
II's strips, being based on a sequence of 'natural' curves fitting the contours
and features of the ground. Commentators remarked on the more picturesque situations that Scottish houses usually enjoyed, compared with their
English counterparts, even if they were not always so well exploited.
Spottiswoode, sadly, was not well endowed with natural features, but lay
on the gentle slope of the vast expanse of Lammermuir, the only water
being a hill burn half a mile to the west.

Neither John II nor John IV, then, had much to guide him in planting
the estate. Both had to impose shape on amorphous surroundings. But
where John II's planting was based on a very human and practical desire
for enclosure, John IV aimed at creating the illusion of a naturally wooded
landscape. This was successful as far as the woods go, but some of the
great stone dykes that curve their way across the hillside seem more the
product of a pencil on a map than an eye on the ground.

The earliest Ordnance Survey of the district made in 1856, towards the
end of John IV's life, clearly shows the enormous extent of his 'natural',
i.e. irregular, planting, superimposed on the remains of John II's strips.
Crawford's less accurate map of 1843 shows just as dense a pattern, while
that of Sharpe, Greenwood & Fowler in 1826 shows the planting reaching
out along the roads and boundaries as the estate was progressively
enlarged and enclosed. Within the boundaries, coverts of amoeba-like
form took shape, some of which survive to the present. Even given the
devastation caused by commercial forestry after 1935, the general outlines
of John IV's scheme can still be seen, and its civilising effect on the
landscape is in strong contrast to the bleak expanse of Greenlaw Moor to
the east.

All this was a process that was repeated many times as Scottish lairds
sought to make their domains resemble the parks of their English peers,

with whom they were increasingly intermarrying. However, by the time
the new Spottiswoode House rose above the trees in 1834, new tendencies
in Scottish gardening were making themselves felt. John IV's woods were
very well at some distance, but for the immediate surroundings of the
house something more formal was required. Sir Walter Scott in 1827
praised the formal terraces that fronted Balcaskie House in Fife, remarking
that 'the beastly fashion of bringing a bare ill-sheared park up to your
very door seems going down'. These terraces were made on the advice
of William Sawrey Gilpin, the English landscapist and student of the
picturesque, who also advised the Duke of Buccleuch on new surroundings
for Bowhill. Balcaskie was near to John's grandmother's old house of
Charleton, and Bowhill was of course the family home of his future
son-in-law, Lord John Scott. So although we are cheated of any evidence
about John IV's professional advisers, it is quite clear in what circles his
ideas would have originated.

It was no surprise, then, that Spottiswoode was also fitted up with a
terrace, the length of which, 300 feet, was considered extraordinary.
The pavilions of John II must have been destroyed by its construction. The terrace commanded a view over the new woods to the Cheviots
many miles distant, a view which also took in a new artificial loch in the
middle distance. Below the terrace but to one side lay a formal garden,
of the kind then becoming popular once more. Some details of it survive,
but its full intricacy can be seen in the 1857 Ordnance Survey. No doubt
the garden was developed over a long period. There seems to have been
a wave of improvement shortly before, or after, John IV's death in 1866.
Several estate houses were built after the 1856 survey. The home farm
cottages were replaced or rebuilt, and bear a datestone of 1860. It was
about this time that the estate adopted a uniform style of subsidiary
building, with whinstone walls and wide sandstone dressings, overhanging
eaves and lattice windows. It was a belated gesture towards the picturesque
imaging of the country estate as a total work of art, an organism whose
every manifestation served the taste and displayed the status of its owners.

As in the late eighteenth century, there seems to have been a period
of growth just when the controlling hand of a long-time Laird was

weakened by age, then removed by death. John IV was 86 when he died on 5th July 1866. His widow, Helen Wauchope, survived until 1870, when their daughter Alicia Anne at last became châtelaine of the estate. So whose was the initiative behind these changes? We learn from Margaret Warrender's Memoir of Alicia that John IV's unmarried and masterful sister-in-law, Jean Wauchope, was often at Spottiswoode and was accustomed to making changes in the Laird's absence. But they probably did not extend to building houses. The picturesque cottages, such as those on the A679 at Dod Mill, easily suggest Alicia's taste, but some were built before she took over. In the absence of all the later estate papers we shall never know who provided the continuity; all we can say is that the nineteenth century was a century of continuous improvement at Spottiswoode. 'His own estate', noted Margaret Warrender of John IV, 'was admirably managed.' The tradition lived on and right up to the time when it was finally dispersed the estate is said to have been beautifully kept.

10

The Wise Woman
of Spottiswoode

WHEN John Spottiswoode IV died in 1866, the future of Spottiswoode, like that of country estates all over Britain, must have seemed immutable. The events that would shake their foundations fifty years later were already preparing, whether he knew it or not. More immediately, as he must have been painfully aware at his death, John had failed to secure the succession of a male heir of his body to the estate. The eldest son, the intended John V, had died unmarried in 1846. The next son, Andrew, married rather late and had a son John, who died in infancy, and then a daughter, Helen. John IV had three daughters, of whom one also died in infancy. The eldest, Alicia Anne, who seems to have been very close to her father, married in 1836 Lord John Montagu Douglas Scott, younger brother of the 5th Duke of Buccleuch. Her marriage ended in sorrow when he died, childless, in 1860. The next daughter, Margaret Penelope, married in 1834 the boy next door, in the person of Hugh Hume Campbell, heir to the baronetcy of Campbell of Marchmont. But again tragedy struck: she died in 1839, having given birth to just one child, Helen Hume Campbell. It can have been little comfort to John IV that he had had at least sixteen cousins in his own generation. The all-important male succession to the name and estate of Spottiswoode of that Ilk, with all that that implied of loyalty to the place, had been broken. At his death, John was survived only by one daughter, and two granddaughters, both named Helen.

When John came to make his final will in 1863 'in consequence of the

lamented death of my last surviving son Colonel Andrew Spottiswoode'
(he died on 12 August 1862), only one of his granddaughters was married.
Helen Hume Campbell had married George Warrender, heir to the baronetcy of Lochend, a fellow Scottish landowner. She was twelve years
older than her cousin Helen Spottiswoode. But as the child of a son, it
was the unmarried Helen who took precedence in the succession, after
her aunt Alicia Anne. Eight years later, Helen Spottiswoode married an
Anglo-Irishman, Captain Charles Herbert of Muckruss. Captain Herbert
was from an Irish branch of one of the grandest families in England, the
Herberts of Wilton, Earls of Pembroke. But from the point of view of
the estate, it was a knell, for the Herberts had no interest in Scotland.
There is some suggestion that there was tension between Spottiswoode
and the Warrender family, who might have felt with some justice that
the estate would have been safer in their hands, and who were obliged
to witness its final breakup two generations later. It was a descendant of
Helen Hume Campbell who gave us our only account of Spottiswoode
as it was in the time of John IV and his daughter Alicia Anne (*Songs and
Verses by Lady John Scott*, edited with a Memoir by her grand-niece
Margaret Warrender, Edinburgh 1911).

Meanwhile, on the death of John IV's widow in 1870, Spottiswoode
entered thirty years of tranquillity under its most famous occupant, Alicia
Anne, Lady John Scott. She was by that time a widow of 60 years of
age. Alicia was the stuff of which legends are made, so much so that she
has impressed herself on later generations as the fount of all that is
interesting about Spottiswoode. It has been part of the purpose of this
book to correct the imbalance, and to show that Spottiswoode reached its
modern form before her day. But the history of early Spottiswoodes is
dry stuff compared with the romantic memory of the solitary, sentimental,
strong-willed, hard-riding, nature-loving Lady of Spottiswoode. Hers is
the ghost, seen or imagined, that haunts Spottiswoode and the other places
where she lived. Her regal if eccentric ways are still remembered, her
harp, her antiquities, her music are national treasures, the remains of some
of her arbours can still be seen, the stone where Lord John proposed
marriage is still pointed out. Her spirit lives in the windswept expanses

of bentgrass on the Lammermuirs she loved, as well as in her pretty Victorian garden. It is unfortunate that Alicia was so reluctant to have her portrait taken. There is an early idealised head of her by Chalon, which tells us little. On the fly-leaf of her album of music in the National Library of Scotland is stuck a photograph of a heavy broad-faced woman in late middle age, dressed in black, which is not captioned and which can hardly represent a lady of her standing. It seems to have been over-looked that there exists a very early calotype by Hill and Adamson, identified as Lady John Scott (catalogue of the Hill and Adamson calotypes in the Scottish National Portrait Gallery, by Sara Stevenson, repr.). Considering what we know of her character and habits, it shows a surprisingly demure and rather pale-faced slim young woman, plainly dressed and studiously reading a book. This was probably taken about 1843, possibly outside Caroline Park.

Thanks to the loss of all the more recent Spottiswoode records, we cannot know exactly how Alicia altered the appearance of the estate. She must have developed the garden, turning it gradually from the formality the 1835 house would have dictated, into the sheltered Victorian garden whose ruined features can still be seen today. Her niece by marriage, Mrs John Herbert-Spottiswoode, continued her practice of planting and spreading bulbs through the policies. Alicia was presumably responsible for the enormous peach house, a late addition, from which fruit was still being given free to local people even after the demolition of the house. This would have pleased Alicia who, like many a Victorian lady with a conscience, was also a philanthropist. It is said that no-one looking for work on the estate was ever turned away. A more picturesque tale has it that she disguised herself to observe her guests coming through the lodge gates, to see what they gave to the people begging there, and might later confront them with their meanness. Perhaps they were not really beggars at all but the numerous family of the lodgekeepers, used to exacting a small charitable toll from the gentry. Like most of the tales told of Alicia, this one can never be corroborated.

It is quite likely that Alicia Anne, long before she inherited the estate, was influential on the way things were done. She certainly began to collect antiquities from the estate and surrounding country well before 1870. This aspect of her life, at least, is well documented, for her collection eventually passed to the National Museum of Antiquities and was professionally catalogued. It consists of flint arrow heads, stone and bronze axes, and cinerary urns, as well as more recent antiquities. One is astonished, in this depopulated country, not by the evidence of early man in Berwickshire, but at the many sharp eyes of Spottiswoode men turning the soil, seeing something unusual and knowing where to bring it, no doubt for a reward. There is some suggestion that Alicia sometimes allowed her romantic imagination to run away with her, as when she excavated a stone circle, not realising that it had been erected by her great-grandfather, John II. The finding of stone cysts in the Twinlaw Cairns which Alicia reported in 1870 her father had found (though she did not claim to have been there) was contradicted later by an eye-witness (Historical Monuments (Scotland) Commission, *Inventory of Monuments etc. in the County of Berwick*, p.52). It has been suggested that Alicia bought old portraits in order to attach Spottiswoode identities to them. This is rather implausible. There is always uncertainty about the authenticity of very early portraits, and speculative identities exist in the oldest family collections. There is no reason for doubting the identity of the surviving portraits of Archbishop Spottiswoode and his son, Robert. The sparse number of family portraits in the 1935 dispersal sale does not support the idea of Alicia's romantic duplicity in that respect, although the portrait of the mediaeval Sir John referred to below must be a reconstruction of some sort.

Be all that as it may, there is no doubt that Alicia Anne Spottiswoode was a romantic to her heart's core. There was a serious and a less serious side to her romanticism, but in that age they were not always kept pedantically apart. The less serious side shows itself in these and many other anecdotes. But how do we class the physical traces of her romantic fancy? In the ruined policies of Spottiswoode, there is a stone cell a yard or two in each direction, fronted by huge boulders, piled up in such a way as to form a small opening. But in the side, hidden by bushes, there is a little wooden door. Had it been larger, it might have been the door to a pretended hermit's cell. Possibly an animal was kept in it, but family tradition suggests that Alicia used to enjoy putting her finds there, to be 'found' all over again by unsuspecting visitors. This would be consistent with what Margaret Warrender recounts, that Alicia used to organise elaborate surprises for children in the shape of planted 'treasure' while living at Caroline Park at Granton. True or not, we cannot assume that the 'hermit's cell' at Spottiswoode dates from her time because she used it; the fashion for such things predated her by several generations.

Another piece of tangible evidence of Alicia's fancies is her harp, now in the Royal Museum of Scotland. Characteristically, it is an imaginative recreation, neither a modern instrument nor an exact replica of an ancient one. In fact its design and construction are, like herself, eccentric, and are probably the result of Alicia's instructions to the estate cabinet-maker. Since the instrument cannot now be tuned, an appeal was launched in 1991 by Marianna Lines, a descendant of Governor Spotswood now living in Scotland, for funds to make a replica in playable order. She is also the author of a one-woman play about Alicia performed at the Borders Festival of that year.

The harp was no doubt used by Alicia to accompany her singing, try out her settings of old tunes and assist her in the composition of new ones. When the harp was presented to the Museum in 1931, it was said to have 'hung in the hall at Spottiswoode for fifty-one years'. At that date Alicia had been dead for thirty-one years. Had she hung up her harp some twenty years before her death, or was it simply hung there when not in use? Alas, the reported statement, as so often, is so ambiguous as to be useless as a clue to the date of the harp. Lady John did of course also have a piano, if not more than one. One, bearing her name, is still in existence in Berwickshire. We cannot know her skills as an executant on either instrument. As a writer of music, we have more evidence of her capabilities, but even here it is difficult to disentangle her own contribution from the traditional airs she noted down, or even from the assistance she may have had from professional musicians of her own day. Her own great gift was to render the primitive emotions and direct speech of the Border tradition into a form to suit the romantic Scotticism of Queen Victoria's age. She herself had a foot, so to speak, in both periods of history, being steeped in the tradition and lore of the Borders, and having inherited in full measure the physical toughness and independence of thought of her Spottiswoode ancestors, yet subscribing to all the more refined *mores* of her own day.

Margaret Warrender may minimise the hoydenish side of Alicia in favour of representing her as a finished Victorian lady, but she does give a fascinating account of her many-sided life. The finishing process, under the benign eye of John IV, went rather against the grain, but she was devoted to her father and willingly adopted his interest in antiquity and natural history. Her poems in French and Italian show that she had learned these languages well enough to use them, in later life, to give her thoughts a different sound. As we shall see, these were more often melancholy than not: (*La voce amata si tace per me*). The family's annual journeys to London, by coach or by sea, made an unforgettable impression on young Alicia, but she could never see London as a second home as John IV did, and was always anxious to go home to Scotland as soon as possible. Her 'coming-out' in Scotland was eased by the cover provided by her extended cousinage. Warrender notes some of the enormous circle of landed families to whom the Spottiswoodes were connected by marriage or descent. Alicia's youthful rides across the Lammermuirs to visit cousins in East Lothian formed her habit of quartering the country in later life, when she would travel by coach to Bowhill and back again in the same day.

At her first ball, Alicia had many partners, aristocratic as well as lairdly. As time went on the distinction between these two classes was effaced by more frequent intermarriage. Both Spottiswoode sisters, in fact, married into aristocratic families, as already noted.

Warrender does not say how or where Alicia met her husband John Montagu Douglas Scott, only brother of the then Duke of Buccleuch. The 'popping stone' where he proposed to her (or, as some say, where she proposed to him) stands beside the back road from Westruther to Spottiswoode. The pair were married in the drawing room of John IV's great new house on March 16th 1836, and went the same day to Bowhill. This marriage propelled Alicia into the highest rank of society. Six years

John Spottiswoode of that Ilk. (1711-1793). Painting attributed to William Denune, *c.* 1740. *Courtesy of Mr Alvin Lines, Atlanta, Georgia.*

Window with the arms of Spottiswoode and date 1596. Spottiswoode West Lodge, reputedly removed from a town house of the Spottiswoode family. *Courtesy of Geoffrey Quick.*

ABOVE: The Groom's House and stable yard, 1770s? (After post-war conversion and removal of central cupola.) *Courtesy of the Royal Commission on the Ancient and Historical Monuments of Scotland.*

LEFT: Painted tracery on gable of west wing of stable yard. *Courtesy of Geoffrey Quick.*

ABOVE: Old Spottiswoode House adapted as annexe to the new house of 1834 (left). *Courtesy of John Herbert-Spottiswoode.*

BELOW: The Spottiswoode Ox. Painting by Alexander Nasmyth, signed and dated 180(1?). *Courtesy of the Royal Museum of Scotland.*

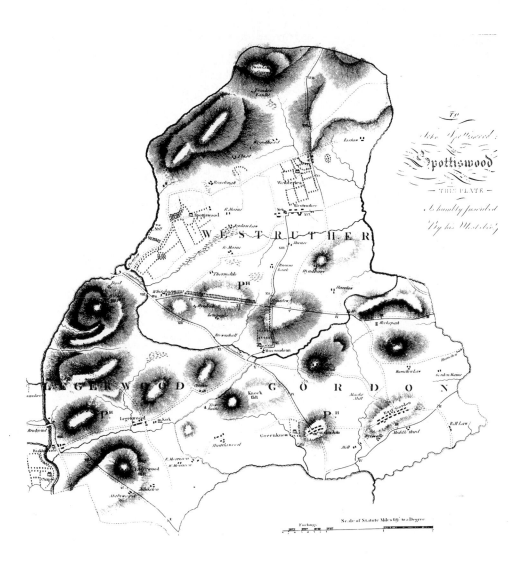

Page from *The Grand Caledonian Atlas* (1805), dedicated to 'John Spottiswood of Spottiswood', showing Spottiswoode within Westruther parish.

1753
page 9.

James Watson Gardner at Duns   Cr
                                                                £ s d

March 16: By Thirty Two & a half days of his son Valentine
           at 6ᵈ p diem with his meal. - - - - - - - - - - - - - - - 16. 3.

1753   By 32½ days of himself at 1ˢ/ p diem wᵗ his meal.   1 12 6
            By five days of himself - - - - - - - - - - - - - - - - -   5. -

July 18   By Two days of himself at the Fruit Trees - - - - - -   2. -

Octᵣ 20   By 1 day -   1. -
Novᵣ 1ˢᵗ   By Three days Shakeing out yᵉ divisions & Strips for plantᵍ
           =ing in yᵉ Wester or paddockhall park - - - - - - - - -   3. -

1754
April 13. By 49½ days from 1ˢᵗ Janʳy last to this day both inclusive th.. 2. 9. 8.
May 25   By 6 days from Monday 20 may to Saturday 25 both included 6. -
Augt 13.   By two days - - - - - - - - - - - - - - - -   6. - -

1755
April 16   By 6 days - - - - - - - - - - - - - - - - -   7. - - -
May 23   By 7 days - - - - - - - - - - - - - - - - - -   7. - - -
July 24   By 1 day - - - - - - - - - - - - - - - - - - -   1. - -
Octᵣ 25   By 2½ days - - - - - - - - - - - - - - - - -   2 6
Decᵣ 20   By 1½ days - - - - - - - - - - - - - - - - -   1 6.

1756
march 10ᵗ By 3 days - - - - - - - - - - - - - - - - - -   3. -
April 17. By sixteen days to the first of May - - - - -   16. - -
           By Wᵐ Turnbull - - - - - - - - - - - - - - - -   7. -
           By 1 Libb Turnept lost of cor - - - - - - - -   9.
           By 5 forlets Bran - - - - - - - - - - - - - -   4 2.
           By 2 Garden Siths - - - - - - - - - - - - - -   3 6
           By 26 Libb pease at 2ᵈ p Libb - - - - - - - -   4 4.
           By 4 Libb Red Clover at 5ᵈ - - - - - - - - - -   1 8.

3 July   By 2 ouc Turnep & 1 oc Radish - - - - - - - -   4
           By 56 Libb Red Clover - - - - - - - - - - -   1. 3. 4.
           By 1 Libb field Turnep - - - - - - - - - - -   3½
           By 6 days to the 3ᵈ July - - - - - - - - - -   6. -
           By the Bell & Custom for the Butter at Duns - -   4

5. Octᵣ   By his son John 2 days - - - - - - - - - - -   1. -
3 Novᵣ   By my self 5 days - - - - - - - - - - - - -   5. -
17.57 Janʳy 10 By 11½ days - - - - - - - - - - - -   11. 6
12 March   By 12 days - - - - - - - - - - - - - - -   12. -
24 —   By 6 Garden Spades - - - - - - - - - -   18. -
14 Apr   By 11 days - - - - - - - - - - - - - - -   11. -
           By 24 Libb white pease - - - - - - - - -   4. -
3 June   By 10 days - - - - - - - - - - - - - - -   10 -
                                                    ————————
                                                    13. 12 7½

1753
10.   James Watson Gardiner at Dunse   Dr
                                                                    £ : : 8

March 16. To Cash . . . .   2. 8. 9.
Novr. V To Cash . . . .   11. —
1754 May 25 To Cash . . . .   1. 1. —
Decembr 28 To Cash in powd of 1/2 doz Silver Tea Spoons . . . .   10. 6.
1755 Novr 29 To Cash in pow'd of 1/2 doz Silver Tea Spoons . . .   2. 6
1756 March 30 To 2 Bowls Turning 1. 13. 7 1/2
      Apr 24 To 4 Stone 3 1/2 Libs Salt Butter at 6 D Lb wibt . . . 1. 16. 1. —
      Jully 3 To Cash . . . .   7. 6.
             To 1/2 lbl Green Tea in a Cannister . . . . .   3. 7. 6.
             To Cloth Sold him in april 1757 . . . . . .   5. . .
             To 1 Libt Chocolate . . . .   1. 6.
             To mending 1 Watch . . . . . .   16. 8.
             To 1/2 dozen Silver Tea Spoons . . . . . .   4. .
             To Turnipe Seed . . . . . .   1. 11.
             To Cash due at Last Compting . . . .
         .. To 1 Horse from Mr Cunninghame in Humbie . .
                      Jas Watson   Cr
                                                            £ s   8.
         By Ballance from ye 94th page 13. 12. 7 1/2
30 Jully 1757 By 3 days . . . .   3. — —
         By 2 Syth Stones . . . . 10.
  3 Octr By 4 days . . . . .   . 1. —
29 Apr 1758 By 6 days . . . . .   . 6. —
13 May — By 2 days . . . .   . 2. —
14 Jully By 1 day . . . .   . 1 —
30 Septr By 3 days . . . .   . 3. —
23 March 1759 By 10 days . . . .   . 10 —
24 April By 2 days . . . .   . 2. —
         By Horse Hire . . .   . 1. —
11 May — By 2 days . . . .   . 2. —
         By 1 Libt Whinn Seed . . . .   1. 6.
         By Setts with Carts at Dunse . .   1. 3. —
21 Jully By Setts with Carts at Dunse . .   . 2. —
  24   By Two days . . .   . 2. —
10 Novr   By measuring the Flax house . . . .   . 2. —
         By 3 days . . .   . 3. —
         By Horse Hire . . .   . 2. —
         By Wm Turnbull 1 knill qs Seeds & plants 13 —
         By Ballance due Jas Watson & paid this
             10 novr 1759   15. —
1764 11 May paid him the accot preceding this   15. 19. 2 1/2 15. 19. 2 1/2
         date & took his discharge at the foot of the
         acco.

23

John Paterson

		O[r]		C[r]		
		£	s	d	£	s	d

1756
March 22: By Ballance due him at Mart[mas] 1746 — — — — 12. 4. 6
By Nine years wages due from Mart[mas]
1746 to Martimas 1755 inclusive at £3
Ster[ling] yearly &c. — — — — 27. — —
By Two Bells made out by Jo Giles — — — 3. 12. 8
By Cloth Cheeses &c — — — — 1. 9. —
By Prin[c]e's board wages allowed to me — — 2. 10. —
To 1 Bill on Ja[s] Henderson 1[st] June 1747 — 5. — — 46. 16. 2
To Corn pease & other as p[er] Acc[t] — — 11. 12. 1.
1753 To 5 firlets of Bear — — — — 13. — —
18 Ap[ril] 1754 To 5 firlets D[itt]o — — — — 14. 8
1755 To 3 Bol[l]s one firlet of Bear at 8[s] p[er] Boll — 1. 6. —
1756 To 4 firlets of Bear — — — — 10. —
To 3 sheep sold at different times — — — 10. —
o 2 Stone 2½ Libb owl at 5[s] p[er] Stone inde. — 10. 8½
o ½ Stone Black owl — — — — 3. —
Ballance due to him over on this 22[nd] 9
March 1756 — } 25. 16. 8½
46. 16. 2.

eod: die Nota I owe John Paterson £10 10[s] Ster[ling] beside
the above ballance, is of rent since y[e] 30 June
1755 the day I received it from the heirs of
Mr Veitch late Min[ister] at Swinton   John Spottiswood

17 Dec[em]r To Precept on W[m] Kirkwood — — — — 5. — —
1757 7 Sep[t] To 200 Herring — — — — 1. 4
21 De[c] 1758 To W[m] Kirkwood for you — — — 5. — —
To 13 Litt Wol at 6[s]8[d] p[er] Stone 1757 — — 5. 5
To 8 firlets of Bear at 12[s] at 5 firlet 13[s] de. — 19. 2
To 3 herlets D[itt]o mar[ke]t last — — — 18. 9½
To 1 firlet Potatoes in 1757 — — — 1. 2
To 1½ firlet D[itt]o 1758 — — — 1. 6
To ½ Stone unsmeared wol 58 — — — 4. —
To 13 Litt Smeared owl at 6[s]4[d] p[er] stone — 5. 5
To 1 Leg of Veal — — — — 5.
To Leg[s] D[itt]o — — — — 4½
12. 8. 9½

116   Robᵗ Wadderston from Chappel at   £ s d   £ s d
Whitby last. He was a Soldier & was 9 years   Dʳ   Cʳ
in North America & has the Chelsea pension.

		£	s	d		£	s	d
Jully	To ½ stone Wool shearing 1770		.	3	6.				
	To ½ English Wool		.	4					
	To 1 English Tup exclusive of yᵉ Skins it was								
	return'd to me & I sold it at Dalkeith for		.	15	—				
	To his share of the Hay bought at yᵉ Coup		.	15	6.				
	To his Cows Grass in ½ Pad: park from Whit 70 to W 71		4	.					
	To His House rent due at Whit 71		.	10	—				
	To His acre first Crop 71		1	.	5				
	By 115 days ½ from 2 April to 31 Decmʳ 1770 at 8ᵈ						3	19	10.
	By his share of Culling the Hay Crop 70						4	.	.
	By His Weeding of Nurserys & Hedges & Cutting &c						4	10	—
	By his fourth share of planting 33,500 firs in 70								
	at 18ᵈ ⅌ Thousand							12	6.
14 Janᵞ 1771	By His Kitchen in Harvest 70						.	2	—
	To the Stripe below Jo Neil's house the								
	length of the gate at Pad: park Crop 70		.	5	.				
21 march	To Cash		1	.	—				
1 Jully	To ½ stone Smeared & 1 ½ stone unsmear Wool 1771		.	10	—				
	To ½⅌ pelled potatoes 3ᵈ & Tred pork Crop 70		.	4	6				
9 Octᵣ	To Cash to His Widow He dyed Sunday		2	2	.				
	1ˢᵗ Septʳ of a fever very much regreted								
	He was an understanding Workman &								
	had been a Soldier was at the Taking of								
	the Havanna & 9 years in Canada & was								
	a Chelsea pensioner.								
27 Decᵣ	To Cash to Jaˢ Newal Wool		.	3	6				
	By his share of Mowing Hay Crop 71 at 20⌀⅌						.	10	10
1772. 23 Janᵞ	To Cash allowed to Jaᵐ Simeeson for Jaˢ								
	Brown Smith on your Husbands Bill		3	6	3				
1773. 24 May	To ½ stone Wool shearing 72		.	4	—				
	To 1 Cows grass to Whit 72 in paddow park		4	.	—				
	House at Whit 72 10ˢ acre Crop 72 & 1 Stripe 5		1	15	—				
	Carryed to the next page		15	3	3		10	15	8

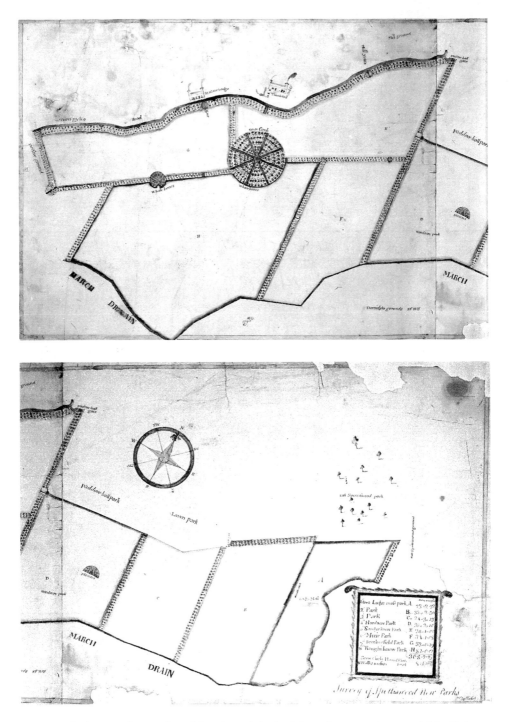

Two recently discovered estate plans of Spottiswoode in the eighteenth century. *Courtesy of John Herbert-Spottiswoode.*

Alicia Anne Spottiswoode, Lady John Scott. Calotype by Hill and Adamson, 1840s. *Courtesy of the Scottish National Portrait Gallery.*

Map of the Spottiswoode Policies. Reproduced from the first Ordnance Survey, 25 in. to 1 mile, 1857. *Courtesy of the National Library of Scotland.*

ABOVE: Spottiswoode House, by William Burn, 1834 (demolished 1938). *Courtesy of Major General Sir John Swinton.*

BELOW: The demolition of new Spottiswoode House, 1938. William Burn's gable ends for the old house, soon to follow it, are on the left. *Courtesy of the Royal Commission on the Ancient and Historical Monuments of Scotland.*

ABOVE: The stable yard with John Herbert-Spottiswoode's Sopwith Pup and estate vehicles. Undated photograph, after 1919. *Courtesy of John Herbert-Spottiswoode.*

BELOW: The tea-house on the island in Spottiswoode loch. Undated photograph, 1920s? *Courtesy of John Herbert-Spottiswoode.*

ABOVE: Mrs Herbert-Spottiswoode cooking trout(?) on the island. Undated photograph, 1920s? *Courtesy of John Herbert-Spottiswoode.*

LEFT: The peach-house, Spottiswoode (now ruinous). Undated photograph. *Courtesy of John Herbert-Spottiswoode.*

later, she was one of the crowd of noblemen and high dignitaries, and
their ladies, who waited on Queen Victoria and Prince Albert on their
visit to Scotland in 1842. As sister-in-law of Buccleuch, she was at Dalkeith
Palace when Victoria and Albert stayed for a week before going on to
the Highlands, and was present at their more intimate occasions. Her
account of these events, reprinted in Warrender (pp.27–32), is rather
breathless with the excitement of it all, but she finds space to express
melancholy thoughts on the Jacobite history of places in Edinburgh the
Royal party visited.

Alicia's Jacobitism can already be detected; she knew that Victoria
represented the line of the Usurper, but consoled herself with the belief
that the Queen herself was a little of a Jacobite. By Alicia's time, the
dynastic issue had no longer anything to do with real power; she could
safely be a Jacobite and refer to Victoria's ancestor as a 'German Hog'
(*We've lookit for ye lang*, Warrender, p.153) without any real disloyalty
to the Crown. I am not sure whether her father would have felt quite the
same. As we have seen, the Spottiswoodes did not declare for the Stuart
cause in 1745, while her mother's family, the Wauchopes, on the other
hand, did.

Covert Jacobites or not, the nobility of the Lothians and Borders
gathered to meet the young Queen, and Alicia was among them. I am
not sure whether this was the first occasion when she was presented to
the Queen: as her husband and brother-in-law both had seats in Parliament, and her father was often in London, this may already have
happened. There is supposed to have been a friendship between them.
Their lifespans were similar, and both were widowed early and withdrew
after that from much society. Even in Lord John's lifetime, Alicia was
not a society lady by preference. She disliked London, and we do not
hear much of Edinburgh, though the couple spent much time at Caroline
Park at Granton, a half-hour's walk from the Capital. Later, Alicia had
a house in George Square there. From her marriage in 1836 until she
inherited Spottiswoode in 1870, it is hard to say where Alicia's real home
was, if it was not the parental one. She started her married life at Cowden-
knowes, but her favourite seems to have been the small house, Kirkbank,

at Eckford, which the Duke granted them. They also used Newton Don and Stichill, both near Kelso. All these houses were in Scotland and, except Caroline Park, all in her beloved Borders. Besides these, Alicia and her husband would have been known and welcomed in very many more, and from her habit of constant riding and driving, she knew the Border country intimately. So perhaps we may say the whole Borders was home enough to her. Children would have anchored her more firmly in one place, but she remained childless.

The fly in the ointment, for Alicia, was her husband's English estate, Cawston, near Rugby, one of the fiefdoms of the old Dukes of Montagu. She did not much like spending time in England, but in fact she was lucky, for the house was ancient rather than grand, had been neglected and needed loving, and had the sort of informal approach and gardens that she preferred. She was free to make her walks, bowers and arbours as she did in all her gardens. There, too, she could exercise her pleasurable duties as the 'mother' of her husband's tenants and workers and their families, and she continued to do so after Lord John's death. At least one may suppose she found pleasure in this humane and charitable activity, for she carried it out assiduously at Spottiswoode, among what she called 'her people'. The door of the room where I write must often have been darkened by her appearance with her basket of victuals and tracts. She and Lord John seem to have felt the same way about their dependants, for we find him writing about them from Cawston to Mrs Spottiswoode: 'remember me to . . . poor, poor Mauchline'. This was in 1855. Some years ago a colonial lady of age and distinguished appearance came to this house, which incorporates three of the old estate cottages. She recalled how she last left it as a small child with a scrub of carbolic and a kindly slap on the bottom from her grandmother, to walk the mile and a half back to her own home. The grandmother's name was Grannie Mauchline. At such moments a sudden rush of continuity catches the throat.

As Alicia, Lady John Scott, is known above all as the creator of the song 'Annie Laurie', I must relate again the well-known story of how it came into existence. Annie Laurie was the daughter of Maxweltown House in Dumfriesshire in the late seventeenth century, and she inspired an unsuccessful suitor, William Douglas of Fingland, to write two stanzas, in the second of which he described her as 'backit like a peacock, and breastit like a swan'. The verses remained unknown until they were published in a volume of Scots ballads by Allan Cunningham in 1825. Some time after her sister's marriage to Hugh Campbell of Marchmont in 1834, Alicia came across a copy in the library there, and liked it, but she 'didn't quite like' the lines just quoted. Her squeamishness in this respect reminds us that the code of propriety we think of as Victorian was in place well before Victoria's accession. Although she was only about 25, Alicia had already, by her own account, written the famous tune for another ballad, 'Kempie Kaye'. She thought it would fit the words of Annie Laurie so she adapted them to the contemporary taste and added a third verse of her own. No longer is our Annie 'jimp about the middle', and with a rolling eye. Instead she is white, sweet-voiced and light of foot. In this form the song became immensely popular, but it was published without Alicia's permission and anonymously. Her authorship did not become known until late in the century.

No other song by Lady John ever had the renown of 'Annie Laurie'. But that does not make it the best of her work. Alicia went on writing poetry for at least fifty years more, and the later verses often show a depth of feeling that 'Annie Laurie' hardly hints at. As collected by her great-niece, Margaret Warrender, who grouped them under heads such as Places, Historical, Jacobite, Family, a single thread runs through them all. There is a profound, palpitating devotion to kinship and country, a total identification with the past as she understood it, in which reason, let alone any form of cynicism, had no part whatever. There is no cause to doubt her sincerity when she wrote, of Prince Charles Edward:

> Noble his spirit, untainted his gallantry,
> Worthy the son of a hundred kings
> (*Shame on ye Gallants*, Warrender, p.152)

When faced with the utmost and undeniable reality, as of death or defeat, her muse became tragic, even bitter: 'Cursed be Culloden, blasted for ever'. For Lady John, even parting was a kind of death, and in her extended family, in that age, death itself was not a rare event. Alicia often had recourse to poetry to relieve her emotions: three years after her sister Margaret Hume Campbell's early death in 1839, she even put pen to paper to reprove the Marchmont family for their unseemly cheerfulness (*Your voices are not hushed*, Warrender, p.236). Lady John's language, as she herself confessed, may not always be equal to her intensity of emotion; she reached down words perhaps too easily, and the horsewoman's rhythm of *A Ride over Lammermuir* strikes me now as the more authentic expression:

> The moorcock flies with sudden spring
> From their swift approach on his startled wing
> (Warrender, p.121)

But her evident sincerity, and her unpretentiousness as a writer, except her from literary criticism, and when she wrote at Spottiswoode on the last day of 1872, two years after she had become its sole châtelaine: 'The dead are near, all I most long to see . . . Keep faith with us! Keep faith with us! They cry', we are convinced that this is indeed how she thought of her family and of the past.

11

The End of an
Auld Sang

'KEEP FAITH WITH US': I wonder if Alicia already foresaw that her niece's marriage would result in a breach of this faith. I hope at least she did not foresee the degradation of the estate that was to occur. At first the auguries seemed to be good enough. As we have seen, her niece's husband came from a very good family indeed. He himself had no part in what was to happen, for he died before Alicia did.

Alicia Anne Scott-Spottiswoode, the name she assumed on her father's death as a condition of his entail, died on 12 March 1900, aged 90. On 16 March, amid the blizzardly viciousness of a late Lammermuir winter, her funeral cortège wound its way to the little village of Westruther. Not for her to be buried under a marble effigy in the new church her family had built, but under a plain sandstone slab in the little old kirk, abandoned and already threatened with collapse. An account of the funeral was privately published, and it inspired at least one poem by a local bard, as if people knew that an era had ended. Her will was found to be dated as early as 1883, though she had added fourteen codicils. Its terms show her devotion to the Buccleuch family, for as well as settling a debt to the Duke which Lord John had incurred, to the extent of £6,000, she left him all the contents of Kirkbank, and Stuart and Jacobite relics at Cawston and Spottiswoode. Her niece Margaret Warrender's progeny were also large beneficiaries. To them went the archaeological collection, then 'principally arranged in the Eagle Hall', which later was given to the National Museum of Antiquities. One of them, Eleanor Warrender, was left Alicia's

house in George Square and all its contents. The other side of Alicia's
character, charity combined with strict morals, was also fully expressed
in the will. The pensions being paid to disabled and elderly workpeople
at Spottiswoode were confirmed for their lives. And she left £2,000 in
the hands of local trustees for the benefit of 'the moral and respectable
poor on the estate of Spottiswoode', drunkards and fallen women specifically excluded. Does this match a little oddly with Alicia's well-known
interest in the gypsies of Kirk Yetholm? Her interest in them seems also
to have been shared by Lord John, for a 'wally coo' jug presented to him
by the King of the Gypsies has descended in the family. One account of
Alicia's funeral included the graphic detail that at one point the then King
of the Gypsies, presumably uninvited to the funeral, appeared and leapt
atop the deceased's bier.

Those were the ways in which Alicia's emotions lay. But the estate
went ineluctably to her niece Helen Herbert's child, John Roderick
Charles Herbert, then aged 18. He, as required by John IV's entail, had
to take the name and arms of Spottiswoode, and within weeks matriculated
the arms at the Lyon Court under the name of John Roderick Herbert-
Spottiswoode. In the period immediately following Lady John Scott's
death, Spottiswoode was let. In the year of her death the Berwickshire
Naturalists' Club paid a visit to Spottiswoode, Thorneydykes and Wedderlie. At Spottiswoode they were welcomed by a Mr and Mrs W. H.
Verdin, who had 'newly become tenants', and made a detailed inspection
of the house and gardens. This is the best account we have of Spottiswoode
as it was in Lady John's time.

John Roderick was married for the first time in 1906, but this marriage
ended in divorce in 1915, and he married the same year his first wife's
cousin, by whom he had a son. Later, he married a third time. Unlike
his great-aunt, John Roderick was a modern person. He had a strong
interest in aviation and the early motorcar. He himself owned a Sopwith
Pup aeroplane, with which he is said to have terrorised the traffic in
Princes Street in Edinburgh. An undated photograph in his son's
possession shows this aircraft in the stable yard at Spottiswoode (which
survived), together with an early motorcar, two pedal contrivances, the

family coach and a sedan chair. John Roderick's interest in aviation led him into dangerous courses. He became a test pilot for Avro, worked for Rolls Royce and had contact with Mercedes Benz, all before the First World War. Being both a fluent German speaker and a good actor, he was recruited for the Secret Service, and was apparently able to infiltrate a Zeppelin factory (C. Andrew: *Secret Service*, p.80).

All this was a world away from the ancient pieties of Spottiswoode. There is no evidence that John Roderick did not start off with good intentions towards his new name and estate, except that as early as 1911 he obtained a court order breaking John IV's entail. Unfortunately apart from the perils of professional espionage (which he may have embarked on precisely to avert a financial crisis) he was in danger from two menaces: the speculative nature of the aviation industry and the perils of modern marriage. According to C. Andrew, a failed investment of £10,000 was the reason why he had to sell a part of the estate, but there were also his obligations to his first wife and to his grandmother to whom he paid an annuity. However, it was not for some years more that the first large-scale attempt to sell the estate took place. In 1919, a prospectus of the whole estate was issued by P. & J. Stormonth Darling of Kelso. The extent of it was then 8868 acres, comprising besides the house itself nine farms and the small home farm, the stables, Eagle Hall, East Side, the loch, and 18 or 20 cottages. Much was made of the timber on the estate, extending to 835 acres, and the shooting. A table of game killed on the estate between 1901 and 1916 yields an astonishing total of 92,712 head, including over 40,000 rabbits. If Herbert-Spottiswoode had hoped to sell the whole estate as a going concern, and thus turn round his fortunes, he was evidently disappointed. That was hardly surprising in the changed social and economic climate after 1918. But the farming community, as well as the asset-strippers and speculators, had been alerted. Within the next few years, much of the farming land and a few other properties had been sold away from the estate.

The outlying farm of Kettleshiel had gone even before the prospectus was issued. Westruther Mains went in 1920, followed by Dods and Dod Mill. Flass, Raecleuch and Hindside Hill were sold in 1921, Howlet's Ha' in 1923 and Thorneydykes in 1924. By 1935 the estate had been reduced to 1397 acres, and included only one tenanted farm, Jordonlaw. The rest of the acreage consisted of the grass parks around the policies and their associated woods, the mostly useless land of Jordonlaw Moss, as well as the policies themselves.

On 17 May 1935 the whole of the remainder was put up for auction, on the property, by John D. Wood. The catalogue is subtly different from the prospectus of 1919. The timber, such a feature before, had already been sold. No-one troubled to record the head of game. Instead, there was much more emphasis on the buildings on the estate, most of which were separately lotted. The mansionhouse, described as 'medium-sized' with 'inexpensive policies', was minutely described, with its 24–27 bedrooms and dressing rooms. Fourteen of these had been called 'servants' bedrooms' in 1919 – but meanwhile the wheel of social change had been gathering pace.

Could the reduced estate have been a viable proposition? John Roderick's son thinks it could. As a lad of 16 or 17, he was not consulted about the sale, and now bitterly regrets it. Of course, the estate could not have supported the house with its army of servants. But then the Spottiswoodes had always had other sources of income. Given John Roderick's financial position, the 1835 house was probably doomed. At any event, no gentleman buyer came forward, not for the whole, not for the house with its 107 acres of policies. I have seen no auction records, but in July 1935 the whole thing was disponed to one Thomas Place, from Yorkshire. Place seems to have been an estate-stripper, and working in conjunction with a lawyer in Duns, Mr Deas, he proceeded to sell off the separate lots. Most of the better estate houses passed into private hands and were preserved. The better grazing lands went to various agricultural interests, the less well-drained and the woodland sites eventually to the Forestry Commission. The mansionhouse stood for at least another three years and Place or Deas retained the last foreman, William Baptie, until early 1939. By all accounts Baptie thought himself in a state of siege. His position must have been uncomfortable when a large gathering of farmers, councillors, even a Provost, assembled to break down the barriers that the new owners had erected on the right of way through the park. They were led by Captain A. R. McDougal, a respected gentleman farmer from the near neighbourhood. Addressing the gathering from a vantage point, Captain McDougal lambasted the 'absentee land speculators', and neither locks, nor two minions of the unpopular Deas, could stop the triumphant procession up the Lawn Park and to the West Lodge (*Kelso Chronicle*, May 15th 1936).

Poor Baptie was left to dispose of various outdoor items and even bits of the fabric of the building. He remarked in a letter to the young John Spottiswoode that Deas the lawyer was 'keeping the Atco motor lawn mower for his own use', which somehow seems to typify the man. On 24 April 1939 Baptie writes: 'now as to the Estate you will know a great difference all the trees are cut and there is two sawmills on the job. I expect about another year and they will be finished. Of course the Forestry Commission are planting up. All that is left in my charge is about 100 acres. The mansionhouse is being demolished and everything is in a mess'. Before Christmas he writes again: 'I sold the metal beams and they are busy blasting them out just now'. Given the ambiguity in the phrase 'is being demolished', that places the demolition of the house, for which various wrong dates have been given, between April and December 1938.

In the *Weekly Scotsman* of 15 January 1948, a local antiquary, Walter Brydon, recorded his impressions on revisiting Spottiswoode. Nowhere, he wrote, had he come across a transformation so complete as that which had overwhelmed it. 'As I remember it in my younger days, Spottiswoode was still one of the great showpieces of Scotland. Its magnificent parks, fine roads, close-trimmed hedges, and well-cared-for buildings were as spick and span as a Brigade of Guards on inspection parade . . . All, now, is changed. The great woods exist no more.' Brydon recorded the widely heard but unattested story that the stones of Spottiswoode were used as bottoming for the airstrip of Charterhall, a few miles away in the Merse. This seems quite likely, for it was the time of hasty rearmament. Place may well have been biding his time, hoping that somebody might want the house. Perhaps the Air Ministry, or whatever government department was responsible, made him the best or only offer. That might also account for the even greater vandalism of demolishing the old house along with the new, although it is said that there was a disappointed buyer for it. If he had been older, the young John Spottiswoode would have kept the old house, which he considers could have been the centre of a pared-down agricultural estate. But the same spirit of vandalistic destruction put paid to the Eagle Hall, home to the Spottiswoode Yeomanry and to Lady John Scott's antiquities. There is no record of its demolition, and not a stone of it can be seen. Photographs show a charming building, easily converted into a delightful house, if only someone had had the imagination to think of it. The disappearance of Eagle Hall left the stables (the 'offices') in sole possession of the site. With stabling for thirteen horses, barns and a substantial house, it luckily found a buyer, and for a time was the centre of an antiques business. Later the house was extended into one of the open sheds beside it, the 'shades' of John II, and having been joined in ownership to a large part of the surrounding land, was let to tenants, while the gardens and policies with their buildings, the ice-house, the dovecot, fell progressively into ruin, greatly accelerated in recent years. At the time of writing, the house and stables, the gardens and policies, have been sold to two new private owners who are actively beginning to stem the tide of decay.

The pressures of modern farming leave little over for conservation or aesthetics, or so everyone used to say at times of prosperity for the agricultural industry. Underlying the obvious truism is a deeper reason for the neglect of these things: the old identity of beauty and utility, so evident to John II and even to John IV, has simply been lost. It was clear to the eighteenth century that improvement had an aesthetic as well as a utilitarian aspect. To Lady John Scott, secure in the environment created by her ancestors, aesthetics was more likely a matter of keeping things as they were. But the dereliction of present-day Spottiswoode would have been hateful to her and to her great-grandfather alike. There is fortunately now a different climate of opinion about the claims of conservation, while at Spottiswoode itself improvement is once again in the air.

While the destruction of an estate like Spottiswoode is distressing in an obvious way, the dispersal of the possessions of generations may hardly be noticed. The contents of Spottiswoode were sold on the premises on 29 April 1935, just in time for the house to be cleared before it too was put up for sale. It was a bad time for the art and antiques trade, and prices were generally low. The sale was conducted by Anderson and Garland of Newcastle and lasted three days. The Spottiswoodes were never art collectors, and we know from Lady John Scott's will that she made sure her particular treasures went to family members she thought would appreciate them. No doubt much else had been privately dispersed in that way. We need not regret too much the standardised contents of the numerous bedrooms, which made up many of the twelve hundred lots. But there were family portraits which had not found a home before the sale, which it would be intriguing to see today. The modest and uninformative catalogue attempts no attributions or assessments. What would we make now of the 'Half length portrait of Sir John de Spotyswode, 1368, in armour', with the legend 'He caused build the White Chapel at Spotyswode'? At 46 × 25 inches, on canvas, it was hardly contemporary with the sitter! Perhaps it was this picture that gave rise to the story that Alicia used to buy pretended ancestors. But there were also panel paintings of early Spottiswoodes of possible authenticity, besides seventeenth- and eighteenth-century portraits of men and women who have figured in this narrative. Among them was probably the portrait of John II, now attributed to Denune, which has recently been rediscovered and is reproduced as our front cover. The Scottish National Portrait Gallery took the opportunity to acquire contemporary portraits of the Archbishop and of Sir Robert. But who bought the group portrait of Anne Spottiswoode ('called the Flower of Lammermoor') and of Rachael and John Spottiswoode in a landscape? This conversation piece of three of John II's children would do more to bring the vanished world of Spottiswoode to life than any words can do.

Saddest of all, perhaps, was the fate of the library. Although we saw John II getting rid of at least some of his father's books, the bookish and scholarly habits of generations must have resulted in a unique accumulation of theological, legal and literary source books. No doubt it all seemed supremely irrelevant in 1935. At any rate it proved too much for Anderson and Garland who, at the end, gave up on cataloguing and were reduced to lotting the books in bundles. Just enough information was provided for us to see how much was lost. In fairness to them, it must be said that the best of the library, and no doubt of some other contents, had already been creamed off by Sothebys.

Finally came the bonfires. There is little doubt that sackloads of family papers were burned, but it is not clear whether this was before or after the National Library had assessed them. It is the practice of the National Library to take all of an archive offered to them, and not pick and choose among it. If they did so on this occasion, somebody must have ruthlessly discarded nine-tenths of it beforehand. On the other hand John Spottiswoode believes the Library could have taken more than they did. Among the items that escaped the bonfire and eluded the National Library were the present estate ledger and the set of papers now at Colonial Williamsburg. There were certainly others, which this volume may help bring to light.

From their ancient beginnings in upland Berwickshire, the Spottiswoode family and name have spread to most parts of the globe. For generations now they have lacked a physical focus, something comparable to the hallowed ground, or the seat of a clan Chief, to which people of highland descent so often return. If this book can remind any Spottiswoodes where their roots lie, both authors will feel well rewarded. Inevitably, there is sadness, even anger, at so much destruction, but we are sure there is more to be discovered. Meanwhile, the finding of the estate ledger of John Spottiswoode II, and his portrait, should bring to life the character and achievements of a man who played a forgotten part in the birth of modern Scotland.

PART TWO

The Spottiswoode Diary:
A Commentary

12

The Laird and his Men (I)

IN October, 1753, John Spottiswoode engaged the services of what would now be termed a tradesman or craftsman. His name was William Aitchison and with him were his son, George, his grandson William Midmost and a younger son William junior. They all worked on the estate and, being masons, their work was in stone. The first commission given by the family by John Spottiswoode was the carving of two statues, one of Apollo and the other of Daphne, for which the charge came to £3 13s. 6d. Two years later a second order was placed for two more statues, one of Jupiter and one of Juno – so the quality of the first two must have passed the Laird's approval. Some months later the Aitchison family received a commission for a statue of Venus, with a Pedestal, the cost of these to be £6 3s. 6d.

The Laird also wanted some stone vases hewn, but with five statues already on order it would take William Aitchison senior some considerable time to add these. We must also remember that the tools in use at that time would be constantly wearing and needing to be sharpened. If a chisel broke or became unusable through constant wear, it might take weeks before a replacement could be got. To buy a serviceable tool Aitchison might have to go to Glasgow or even across the Border to Newcastle or Berwick where there would be shipwrights and blacksmiths aplenty. On the other hand, he might be fortunate in buying what he needed at one of the local Fairs, but these only visited their allotted centre once or twice a year and might not have carried such items as chisels. Later on the estate would employ its own smith – but that was far into the future.

Meantime, the two stone vases were duly ordered and were 'To be set up at the gate at ye wester avenue'. The cost agreed was to be £1 5s.

Three years passed before any more orders were placed with the Aitchison family, which gives some indication of how long it took them to carve the statues and vases the Laird had already commissioned. But in October, 1758 the work must have been nearly finished as another order was placed – this time for '2 vases for the back court costing £1 10s.'. A year later came a larger order, for statues of the Four Seasons at 30s. each. But there must have been a misunderstanding somewhere because the Laird had to pay a further 3s. 6d. 'for setting 'em up', as this was not included in the purchase price! Did this follow a measure of dispute, one wonders? If so, the Laird might well have thought he held the advantage, being an important customer and therefore lending force to his side of things. But he wanted to place the statues at the ends of paths and walks because having them would be a mark of prosperity and position. Aitchison, knowing this, would press his point accordingly. This seems borne out from what comes immediately afterwards, as the Laird always added 'as per agreement' when placing his orders. He did this when ordering a statue of a Fawn which William Aitchison was to carve for £2 10s. in 1761. But he seems to have forgotten his own vow of caution because the very next entry reads: 'By ye Pedestall not included in ye agreemt . . . 10/–'.

Then came tragedy which is best described by the Laird himself. He writes: 'By ye stone for Venus broke by Wintrop 4s.'. Only once more does Wintrop's name figure in the Diary and that was when Spottiswoode paid him off through the help of a neighbour. It would seem he was too displeased with him to pay him off direct, enlisting the neighbour's assistance to do it for him.

At the end of 1761 William Aitchison was given more work to do on the estate – this time to carve six vases for the two Pavilions at a cost of 6s. each. But judging from the price, these must have been quite small because only one month later a further four vases were bought at 12s. each. Nevertheless he adds the remark that 'These are bought delivered'!

Then comes a new problem. The kitchen gable end of the house had to be rebuilt because of the 'reek'. This being a craftsman's job, Willie

Aitchison was called in. The entry reads: 'July 5th. 1769. He came here to take down the kitchen chimney'. The work done on it must have been satisfactorily completed because six more vases were commissioned at 12s. per piece.

On 30th May, 1771 old William must have asked for some money because there was, as the Journal relates, '£1 sent him by ye maid's moyr'.

At the bottom of the page another local Fair is mentioned. This time, it was held on 19th November at Duns (or Dunse, as it was then spelt). A tenant 'Brought my Note for £1. 19. 9d., dated 11th. November'. Payment by 'Note' or 'By precept' was a normal way of paying either for goods or services. Actual coinage was extremely scarce and became scarcer through the use of foreign coins. Accordingly, payment by Note or Precept was normal, being a form of promissory note.

When the Union of Parliaments came about in 1707, all Scottish coinage was called in for exchange into Sterling. Scotland did very badly out of this, her specie being devalued down to one twelfth of the English equivalent. The reason was partly due to the Darien Scheme on which Scotland lost so much of her capital, and partly to the general backwardness of a nation with few industries. The total coinage produced for exchange at the Union was only in the region of £60,000 – the value of a large farm today. In addition, there was a whole host of strange coins circulating, some with outlandish names – the bodle, the plack, the dyot; the groat and bawbee; the shilling, the penny and the merk. English traders – the few that there were of them, apart from cattle drovers – fought shy of trying to trade in Scotland because of the scarcity of money. On the other hand, the Highlanders were forced to sell their thin, stunted beasts in order to have enough money to pay the rent and buy meal for the winter. Even though the cattle brought in a mere 10s. to £1 per head, they had to be sold. Otherwise, their owners faced eviction. Naturally, this prevented any opportunity of accumulating capital.

By 1772, William Aitchison was obviously an old man. But the Laird took him into his own house to work there and so keep him out of the wet and cold. This was a kindness, as was the paying of a wage of 1s. 4d. per day, higher than anyone else received on the estate. In addition, the

Laird asked him to carve an unusual statue which he described as follows: 'By 1 Black [i.e. a Negro slave], Bearing a dial on his head set up at the Mason's lodge . . . £1 1s.'.

But this was the last commission William Aitchison was able to undertake. The following year, John Spottiswoode wrote this in his Diary: 'He dyed Friday, 4th June of a tedious illness I regrated him much as he had wrought to me above 20 years. Cutted all my Statutes [sic], Vases and flower pots and done all the best hewn work about the house besides I looked upon him as an honest man well natured and obliging'. Altogether, the Laird had ordered 10 statues and 20 vases for which he paid a total of £31 6s. 6d. One wonders what became of them and where they are now. It is not possible to identify them in the catalogues of the sale of the estate in 1935.

For the most part, the names of tenants and farm servants which appear in the early pages of the Diary have come forward from the missing Ledger C. In other words, they were already settled at Spottiswoode when the present Diary/Journal first opened its pages. We know that James Rutherfoord, William Turnbull, Thomas Henderson and John White were in this category and another was Alex Haig. He was a wright and an important craftsman on the estate. But one of the first entries against his name has a sad ring to it. 'By 1 dead coffin furnished to Jo White's daughter . . . 6/–'. Then comes further evidence of the acute shortage of timber when the Laird sells Haig a large Press of three divisions. At the same time, he bought '2 dales one 10 foot and ye oyr 12 in length'. These would be deals of soft wood, probably conifer, as hard wood would be virtually impossible to find. A further example of this dearth of wood was given by John Cockburn of Ormiston when he sent his gardener Charles Bell a single plank 'to be used with prudence'. Alex Haig was obviously a trustworthy man because just before Christmas of 1757 John Spottiswoode sent him down to the Minister 'to cut his timber for 5 days' and paid him 5s. for doing so.

On 26th December, we have another example of the shortage of coins in Scotland: 'Took up ye old Note and granted him a new one for ye balance being £4. 9. 10d.'.

In 1758 sowing of the cereal crop must just have started or was about to start. It could have been either as the date was 5th April and it is recorded that Haig supplied the Laird 'With a piece of ash for Harrow-rungs and how shaft' – 'how' being Lowland Scots for hoe. Ash, because of its strength, would be used to make the harrow frame, and the actual harrowing of the ground would be done by the rungs or teeth, attached at right angles. At this time, when there were very few farm implements, a gorse bush or a big bunch of ivy might serve as a harrow to bury the cereal seed. In the following year, John Spottiswoode bought a whole ash tree from Alex Haig for 6s. 'to be used to furnish shafts'. Presumably the shafts would be for his chaise, because not until much later did wheeled carts appear on the estate. Owing to the terrible state of the roads, a carriage would take great punishment from ruts, ditches and stones, especially after a wet spell or a severe frost. It took Lord Lovat ten full days to travel from Beauly to Edinburgh and might easily have taken much longer had the army not helped with carpenters and smiths as well as a big team of men to pull his carriage along after the wheels and shaft broke. John Spottiswoode would want the wood of an ash tree, because it was stronger than most other timber available.

An interesting entry follows: 'His son wrought 11 days but he [Alex Haig] charged nothing for him as he is but new gone to work'. The boy was probably only 11 or 12 years old. However, five months later, he was engaged again and this time his father charged 4d. per day for his services!

We now see mention of Flass Wood again and the Diary records that Alex Haig was given the task of cutting timber from it. The Laird would want this carefully done on account of the shortage and Haig was the obvious man to do it. Accordingly, in July 1760, the Laird made this entry in his Diary. It is a most important piece of information: 'By 4 days with his son cutting an opening in ye Flass wood for ye stance of a dry stone dyke, both without meal . . . 6/8'. From this information it would appear that Flass was an extensive plantation and that the Laird 'managed' it in the same manner as the monks had done. They divided each major plot of trees into four sections, each one bordered by a drystone dyke. When the first section was felled, sheep and cattle were allowed in to clean up, after which the area felled was replanted and once more sealed off. The next section was then opened up, ready for felling. A wood so managed grew timber efficiently, ensuring a constant supply. It was just as well since the monks were always in need of timber to build their granges and furnish their monastic buildings. Depending on the area of a wood, it could grow trees indefinitely using this type of management. John Spottiswoode clearly knew about it as his order to Alex Haig indicates in asking him to prepare 'Ye stance of a dry stone dyke'.

Having done as they were bid, the two Haigs, father and son, were asked to make two wheelbarrows and the wooden bodies for two more. These would be quite an innovation in 1760 because wheels of any sort were a rarity, there being few roads, only rutted tracks and therefore little or no trade except in and around the larger towns. Goods were usually conveyed on sledges or tumbrils but also on carts with solid wheels, though these were not popular as they constantly broke or fell off. Goods from the Borders were often conveyed on pack-horses up the Gala Water, the ill-grown beasts finding it easier to carry their small loads along the riverbed rather than up the hill tracks. Although the passing of the Turn-pike Act in 1751 held out the promise of improved communications, it was 20 years later before much improvement could be seen in the condition of the roads. Meantime, such trading as there was continued to be carried by pack-animals. A 'load' of meal, for example, meant two bolls (or 280lbs on average although differences were frequently found, e.g. at Berwick, Duns and Kelso, and at Carlisle, Newcastle and Darlington across the Border. Glasgow stood alone with its Boll of 240lbs).

The Laird must have had confidence in Alex Haig because, as we have seen, he also engaged his son, William. Their wages and conditions varied, of course, William receiving, as well as his pay, a pair of shoes (calculated by the Laird as being worth 2s. 2d.). His younger brother, Sandy, was paid 10s. for the summer and also had a pair of shoes.

Next come several intriguing entries covering the Spottiswoode hay crop. Hay was not greatly regarded in eighteenth-century Scotland and was often cut in awkward, wet places and between stones and then sold by public roup, i.e. by auction. John Spottiswoode obviously decided to have his hay cut under his own eye and then sold. The task of cutting went to Alex Haig who, in 1765, also bought the park hay for £1 3s. 6d., but as he also bought a single rick from the Laird for 5s. 2d., he would surely obtain between four and five ricks from the park hay. There being no comment in the Diary one way or the other, we must assume both sides were satisfied.

Following this comes a further very interesting entry. The Laird buys from Alex Haig a 'Churn-staffe' (the stick used to insert in a churn for making butter) costing 4d. Next, he buys a 'Thorle' (a round perforated stone used as the flywheel of a spindle; but probably the spindle was also included) and a 'Spile' (can mean the plug for a cask or barrel, but perhaps this was in fact the spindle). These small items cost the Laird a mere 8d., but they show the shortage of wood in graphic manner.

By 1766, Alex Haig's three sons were all working to the Laird: William, Sandy and John. As their father died that year, it was as well. But it also shows John Spottiswoode to be a considerate man, although whatever was bought from him, even 'Fir Spurrs for a chimney' costing 6s., had to be paid for, as was 'A cartfull of timber from ye Flass wood' costing 3s.

There were many other transactions with the Haig family, first with their father, assisted by his sons, and then with the three sons alone, after their father died. This shows that they probably lived on the estate, working at day rates except when their knowledge as carpenters was needed. For example, the 'Fir spurrs' were 'for the Baillies house' for which they paid the Laird and then charged the Baillies for them, plus their labour. They also rented a patch of grass to graze four sheep for the year costing 6s. In addition, Haig bought several thousand nails from the Laird, which shows they were either made on the estate or bought in to retail to his tenants. These and similar transactions continue to reflect the shortage of actual money and how dependent the tenants and farm servants were on the Laird.

William Haig, the eldest son, now had a page in the Journal to himself, but he worked on the land more than as a carpenter and was paid 7d. per day. However, after two years doing this the rate was raised to 8d. He also continued to buy nails from John Spottiswoode – 1,000 double flooring nails, 1,000 single ones, 1,500 window nails and 1,500 saddle tacks, from which we can deduce that he carried on quite a substantial business, apart from working as a farm servant on the estate. His two brothers seldom figure, Sandy alone being mentioned and then only when given three months' general farm work, and then he was hired through William. There is further evidence that wheeled carts were used at Spottiswoode, the Laird buying from Will Haig '3 fillies to a cart wheel' and a little later six fillies for another wheel and nine oak spokes for a total of 6s. 6d. There was a sale of timber at Eyemouth, the Laird sending Will Haig over to buy some, reimbursing him for his expenses to the tune of 2s. 7d. It would be a fair ride, by Greenlaw, Duns and Chirnside, some 20 miles of rough and rutted country. But he did succeed in buying some wood although the Diary does not specify how much or at what cost.

As the years passed, Will Haig continued in John Spottiswoode's service, providing him with various carpentering articles. He made more fillies and wheel spokes, and then comes a more surprising item – he sold the Laird five timber chairs for the kitchen. These could have been for the house staff or for some of the young unmarried men who, by custom, ate in the house. He charged the Laird 22 pence for them, which shows they were possibly second-hand. He next made two shafts for paring spades – but more about these later when John Spottiswoode tells us about his experiments with 'paring and burning', i.e. paring off the old sod from untamed land, drying it and then getting rid of it by burning – a slow, laborious job.

In July of 1774, Sandy Haig is mentioned again, but only because 'He left my service' (in July 1768) and was due the balance of his wage, viz. £1 18s. 4d. – a wait of 6 years! It could be, however, that Will had already paid him and was being reimbursed by the Laird.

There were increasing calls for supplies of timber from the Flass Wood, due to more houses and farm buildings being built at Spottiswoode, and Will Haig was always in charge. An example is an entry for July 1774 of his 'Cutting a load of timber from the Flass Wood for Birkhall houses'. Then comes an extraordinary entry – he had overlooked squaring up

Sandy and John for work done in 1773 amounting to 13s.! Needless to say, the question of interest never arose. The next article Will Haig made was 'A spoked hurle barrow wheel', costing 2s. 6d. It must have pleased the laird for he then bought 'One steel to a hurle barrow' costing 6d. A steel was a handle and a hurle barrow was a wheel-barrow. The next entry in Will's account was strange. It ran: 'To cash for the grains of the wood at Gordon . . . 3/–'. The grains were the branches of a tree which were lopped to make it grow. With timber so scarce, even branches were valuable, regardless of shape. Where the wood was at Gordon, the Diary does not say nor does it tell us how the 'grains' were transported. The next entry of note runs as follows: ' By 4 sheths to ye drogue at 4d. each'. A sheth was a stick which a mower used to whet or sharpen his scythe. But a 'drogue saw' is a cross-cut saw which the Laird spelt according to his own wish. A drog-saw was a term peculiar to the south of Scotland and this could explain its use, especially to a craftsman in wood like Will Haig.

Haig's name goes nearly to the end of the Diary – the only one of those who were working at Spottiswoode before it first began. But there are no appreciative remarks as were written when William Aitchison died or when James Rutherfoord left. Instead, he was granted a free house, free of rent for one year and six bolls of meal. In return, 'He was to look after all the tree-planting and do any "wright" work in the House or any other work which needed doing'. He was clearly a good all-rounder whom the Laird could trust. We can trace him as far as 1782, but after that all mention of him stops. There had been a member of the Haig family at Spottiswoode since 1750 – a connection lasting 32 years.

Next among the early band of farm servants, who came into the Diary from the missing Ledger C, is James Rutherfoord. His first transaction with the Laird was the purchase of 'an old Kist' for which he paid 1s. Infant mortality was high at this time (in some areas of the Highlands one child in five died), so this 'kist' might well have been for one of Rutherfoord's children. As can be seen from his first page of transactions, there was nothing remarkable about James Rutherfoord. He had work to do and did it, all in accordance with his bargain with the Laird to work for 6d. per day.

There are two unusual entries – the first reads: 'By his kitchen in time of harvest'. Instead of the Laird providing the reaper's midday meal, he paid him an agreed sum in compensation – in this case 2s. The other entry reads: 'By 3,000 divots casting at 1/– p.m. . . . 3/–'. These were turves of peat or heather, to be used for the man's roof. Sometimes they were supplied by the Laird for nothing, but not in this case. Casting made poor shelter from the elements, gales tearing at it and birds nesting in it, to say nothing of mice and other vermin. The ancient term was 'thayk and dyffat'.

Every now and again, John Spottiswoode charges 1s. 4d. for 200 herring. These must have made a welcome variation to the diet. They would be salted and when eaten with potatoes (which were beginning to form part of the cottar's diet) were quite delicious. The Laird would probably buy herring by the cask and doubtless made a good profit from selling them to his people. He also sold them potatoes, charging them at 12d. per lb, or 112s. per cwt.

On page 29 of the Diary, we find two more interesting entries. The first concerns the purchase by Rutherfoord of '2 capfull of lintseed'. This was a recognised measure in the area, its full name being 'A Kelso capfull'. It is a term seldom come across, but used several times by the Laird. Lint seed would be for growing flax for weaving into hard-wearing cloth. At the bottom of the page the Laird writes: 'Nota. James Rutherford had wrought with me [he writes 'wi' me] at 6d. p. day from Whitsun 1747 to Whits 1760 when he hired as herd at 30/– yearly, 6 bolls meal, 1 cows grass, summer and winter and a free house'.

In the many transactions James Rutherfoord had with the Laird the word 'firlot' frequently appears. This was a measure of grain or meal – in this case oatmeal – and was the fourth part of a boll of 140lbs, i.e. 35lbs, but Teviotdale measure as the Laird points out on several occasions. There is also mention of meal-seed bought by James; this was the outer husk of oats and dust sifted from the oatmeal then steeped and soured to make sowens or flummery. By the sound of it, this very unpalatable mixture would seem suitable for feeding to his own livestock in times of scarcity. But, in fact, it was fed to humans.

Being now the estate herd (shepherd), Rutherfoord would bring in any dead or fallen animals he might find while doing his rounds. He would be supposed to carry these back to the farm steading and report to the Laird what he had found. Farm servants, there or elsewhere, would not all be as honest as that. From time to time, we see how Rutherfoord would buy 'the leg of a calf for 5 pence' as he did in December 1757 and later 'two old ewes for 3/– and one sheep's skin, for 1/–'. The skin would be especially useful, being ideal for a warm outer garment in winter. Not until May 1759 did he buy another skin, which shows how frugal he was.

At Martinmas, 1762, Rutherfoord rented a small piece of ground 'be-west of ye new yard for 4/–'. This would almost certainly be for grazing a ewe or two or where he could keep a few lambs. The system commonly practised at this time was to allow a lamb to suckle its mother for a month only or six weeks at the most. A piece of stick was then secured across its mouth so that it could not suckle and therefore had to find its own feed where it could. As a consequence, lambs were small and stunted and worth very little when marketed. It was also common practice to smear the sheep's fleece with tar, mixed with butter or oil, so that it did not attract maggots. One of the most difficult changes the Improvers had to make was to wean the people away from this absurd system.

In the same year, Rutherfoord is credited with 12s. for 'working wi' ye spade a piece of wet ground in ye hollow of ye Third and Teind Parks being two thirds of an acre'. This must have been hard going, wet ground being difficult to dig and very heavy to lift. Furthermore, a Scots acre, which this probably was, extended to 25% more than an English acre.

Now and again when the Laird engaged a farm-servant he described him as 'entering upon the term'. Term Days are quite different from the ancient Scottish Quarter Days which are still Whitsunday (or failing that May 15th) and Martinmas (November 11th). Added to these are February 2nd which is Candlemas and August 1st which is Lammas. Removal terms or entry terms were quite different and are still May 28th and November 28th.

James Rutherfoord had to ask the Laird for cash from time to time, notably if he was going to a Fair. But generally he did not seem to be interested in money. He came from the missing Ledger C and was owed about £3 in 1752. But by the end of 1764 he owed John Spottiswoode about £1. Three years later the position was unaltered so that after 20 years, neither side owed the other anything. However, we must take into account the wages in kind. After he entered as herd, James Rutherfoord was given 30s. a year as a money wage and was allowed to keep one cow with summer's grass and winter's fodder supplied. But the value of these was set against him, as was his house rent, despite the fact that the record says he is to receive a free house. He also had six bolls of oatmeal which was not charged. It is worthy of note that in neighbouring East Lothian, the top men still only received six bolls of oatmeal per annum as late as 1793, and some were without a money wage at all.

An item which figures regularly in the Diary is the sale of herring to the Spottiswoode tenants and men. These were salted into barrels and the Laird charged 16d. for 200. They were purchased, of course, to try and vary the monotonous daily diet during the winter when the only meat available was salt beef. This was laid down in autumn when the marts were killed. Presumably, the herring would come down the so-called Herring Road from Dunbar by pack animals, travelling by Spott and Lothian Edge across the Whiteadder south of Johnscleuch, heading towards Westruther and Lauderdale (Thomson's *Atlas of Scotland*, 1821). Another type of food which was made available by the Laird was the potato. The Aitchison family frequently bought them at 1s. or 14d. the firlot. But in his *General View of the Agriculture of East Lothian*, published in 1794, George Buchan-Hepburn of Smeaton infers that potatoes had only recently been introduced. Since John Spottiswoode was growing them in 1750/52, this would seem to strengthen further his claim to be an Improver.

Among the more unusual goods which the Spottiswoode men bought from the Laird was 'Owl'. This was possibly oil extracted from crushing linseed, i.e. the seed of the flax plant. This could provide light in a crusie lamp or could be mixed with butter or tar to dress the fleece of sheep.

But the spelling, i.e. owl, might just as easily stem from the local dialect and could refer to wool. This interpretation is supported by the fact that 'owl' was sold by the stone.

By contrast, bere was bought from the Laird all the year round and by most of his people. This is barley, which, when made into meal, was baked into cakes. The Laird spells it 'bear'. It is of a lower quality than the barley for making malt from which whisky is distilled. James Rutherfoord stands out as one who always tried to bring some variety to his family's diet and his purchases from the Laird illustrate this. He buys meal by the boll which differed in weight from place to place. In Teviotdale it was 7 bushels – approx. 314lbs – but in the Border country of Kelso, Duns and Berwick was usually 140lbs. He also buys linseed, as we have seen, and also pease, which was made into a paste by covering it with boiling water, when it was called brose. Although this field crop had a different bushel weight to barley, the Laird enters James Rutherfoord's purchase as calculated in 'corn measure'. Sensibly, he avoids having to explain the difference, which was small in any case. Page 54 of the Diary gives a list of James Rutherfoord's arrangements with the Laird and also how smoothly he does his work. His only relaxation seems to be visiting the local Fairs whenever they come to the district.

However, in November 1765 a completely new sort of transaction takes place. He sells the Laird 52lbs of butter, 21lbs in 1764 and 31lbs in 1765 at 5d per lb. This must have been the produce from his cow, which he bought for around £3, and for which he paid 6s. 8d. per year in grazing rent. Why the Laird would want to buy so much butter is explained lower down on page 73 when Rutherfoord sells him a further 26lbs in 1766, again at 6d. per lb. This time the Diary explains that the butter is for 'smearing' – that is, mixing with tar and spreading over the sheep's fleece, supposedly to protect it from parasites. It was one of those procedures whose origin is lost in antiquity, but was persisted in regardless. All it did was devalue the fleece as the fellmonger had to get rid of the tar before he could sell the wool. It would seem from the amount of butter bought by the Laird that he ran quite a flock of sheep, although the amount of wool shorn each year would amount only to about 1lb per fleece.

We can tell from the entries under his name that James Rutherfoord was a reliable man and one who did his work in accordance with the Laird's wishes. For instance, there is only one line to denote that he had done his job for 388 days, from Spring 1764 to Autumn 1765 and then for a further 50 days after that, taking him to the end of that year. The next year, 1766, is the same – no complaints or criticism – but no praise either! In those days, a bargain was to be kept, regardless of any temptation to look elsewhere. This is highlighted by Grey Graham when he states: 'The price of grain and food and clothing remained almost stationary during the 100 years from 1640 to 1740'. We could add a further 40 years, from what John Spottiswoode tells us.

By the end of 1771, after some 25 years of service, James Rutherfoord is owed about £3 only, and the same amount by the end of 1775. His wage has not changed, but something very interesting has. For the first time in all the entries against his name, the Laird suddenly records having given James Rutherfoord 10s. 'To pay his tailors'. He must have sold some of his own produce to justify spending money on clothes, so would it be butter or clothing (he frequently bought wool shearing from the Laird at 8s. per stone; and he sold more butter to the Laird – two stones this time at 7d. per lb). This is the first sign of prices beginning to rise with the improving trade in Scotland and the urge for more efficient farming.

There is another sign. As the Spottiswoode Estate continued to be improved under the relentless eye of the Laird and as production from it increased, there would be more land available for reliable servants like James Rutherfoord. This would seem to be the case from an entry against his name for 1776: 'To 2 firlots of oat seed – 7/–'. If we assume a firlot of oats to be about 30lbs (it varied according to bushel weight and quality) and that it was sown at the rate of four bushels per acre, then James had half an acre in cereal. With reasonable weather and no incursions by sheep or cattle the yield might have been in the region of half a ton and this would have been invaluable to his family.

There is another indication. In 1775, Rutherfoord drew 10s. in cash from the Laird 'to go to Lauder Fair'. The following year he drew one guinea, but in 1778 he brought it back to 10s. once more. There might have been a reason for this because in April of 1780 there comes a sad little entry:

To cash instantly given him	5/–
To 1 sheet of stampt paper	4/3d
Writing his last Will in favour of Margrt Wadderston, his neice	1/6d
To a load of meal sent to Lauder with him this day when he went to live with his neice	17/–
To 4 firlots of bear sent also	8/9d
He dyed in an advanced age about 15 or 20 days after he went to Lauder	

Balance due James Rutherford's Executors:	£7. 14. 5d.

It was not a great deal after more than 30 years, but it must have seemed much less to his niece as the final instalment was not paid over by John Spottiswoode until February, 1787!

Thomas Henderson was another of the men who joined the staff at Spottiswoode in the early 1750s. However, there is nothing remarkable about him except his name at the top of the page which is beautifully written in copperplate with the following entry: 'To 1 Threave of Oat Straw . . . 8d.'. This meant 24 sheaves of oats or barley straw – i.e. two stooks. Henderson might have wanted such a large quantity to use as bedding for his family, or to feed to a cow. Buying threaves was unusual and does not appear often in the Diary. At that time, the harvest was cut down by using a scythe, or a smooth or serrated sickle. In a good crop the scythe cut nearly twice as much as either of the two sickles, viz. nearly two acres of wheat against one acre of oats or barley. But it never really caught on in Scotland, being liable (as the people thought) to shed the grain. The sheaves had to be measured according to the rules of the district. We therefore find a sheaf in Banffshire was 10 inches in diameter and a sheaf in the Lothians and Angus was 12 inches. It depended on the weather. The damper the climate, the smaller the sheaf, to make it dry quicker.

Thomas Henderson's name does not appear again, but strangely the Laird does not explain why he left, nor does he close his account. He does not even add up his debit or credit columns. Was Henderson on the run? Or did he join a company at a visiting Fair, or was he caught by the Press Gang?

Another name coming forward from the missing Ledger C is that of John White. He was in debt to the Laird when his name first appeared in the Diary to the tune of £2 14s. 4d. However, this was paid off in the normal way of working by the day and at the usual Spottiswoode rate of 6d. per day. There is one curious transaction, however. In November 1755 White buys 10lbs 'Owl' at 5s. per stone, costing him 3s. 1d. But the following year he buys a further 9lbs and pays 3s. 6d.! White had a skill which not too many farm servants had at that time, namely dry-stane dyking. This is interesting as it shows the Laird's desire to establish enclosures at Spottiswoode. This particular dyke was 288 roods long, costing the Laird £9 0s. 4d., which took into account that White had the use of an estate horse and cart to carry the stones. His 288 roods meant he built about 2000 yards, a rood being 7 yards and regarded as a day's work.

The task of mowing and winnowing the hay for the year 1752 was given to White and Turnbull, each receiving 18s. 9d.

It would appear that John White favoured the unusual luxury of the buying of shoes. The cost varied according to the type of shoe the Laird gave as part of a man's wage. But in the case of White, he bought his own at one of the regular Fairs, the Laird advancing the money. Thus we have this for October, 1753: 'To 1 pair shoes in Earlston Fair . . . 1/4d'. White also bought potatoes at 1s. the firlot and malt at 2s. 6d. 'the capfull', and in September 1755 he was given the task of mowing all the hay, which yielded him £1 10s. In November 1756 the Laird gave him 'Cash to buy shoes at Lauder Fair 2/—'. Perhaps to help his financial position with John Spottiswoode, White sold him a 'young stirk' for £1 3s. This term is still widely used in farming today, a stirk being a young beast 12 to 18 months old. In November 1754, he bought a further firlot of potatoes at 6d. This further strengthens the opinion that Spottiswoode was growing potatoes on a field scale, as distinct from his own private garden, as the previous purchase was also in the autumn, the correct season for lifting potatoes. The final transaction left him owing the Laird £6 10s., but the reason why he left is not stated.

William Kyle is next on the Laird's list. He also started work when Ledger C was operating, although there is very little information on him. This is possibly due to someone other than the Laird keeping the accounts and neglecting to enter up all the various transactions. This view is taken because of a sudden change of handwriting both for Kyle and Rutherfoord whose account is on the opposite page. Was John Spottiswoode perhaps in London, as we know he sometimes visited the Capital? In each case the change in writing ends on 31st December 1754 and the Laird's own distinctive hand resumes. 'William Kyle dyed' is the final epitaph on him, and he was owed £5 18s. It is not known whether Kyle had any family – but if so, they could have used the money, especially if there were growing children. However, in accordance with his usual practice, John Spottiswoode was in no hurry to liquidate this debt, taking six years to do so!

Adam Allan had been taken on in March 1753, but did not stay long. The Laird's cryptic reason runs as follows: '21st March, 1757 – Cleared Adam Allan and dismissed him ye work as he had gone of ye work for a moneth in time of last harvest but as he had been sometime at ye harvest work I gave him 4/– sterling over the above balance'. The only other item of note under his name is puzzling: 'by 16 days of ye Brickman at 2 pence more . . . 2/8d'. Was a Brickman perhaps a baker, as brick was a word for a loaf?

On page 23 of the Diary/Journal are some very interesting entries under the name of John Paterson. They run thus: 'By Ballance due him at Martinmas 1746 – £12. 4. 6d.'. Then: 'By nine years wages due from Martinmas 1746 to Martinmas 1755 at £3 ster yearly thus . . . £27'. One wonders why John Paterson was so different from the other workers on the estate and why his account was as much as nine years in arrears? On 22nd March, another balance was struck showing that the Laird owed him £25 16s. 8d. and then a 'nota – I owe John Paterson £10 10 6d. ster besides the above ballance without rent since ye 30th June 1755, the day I received it from the heirs of Mr. Veitch, later Minr at Swinton'. Then for the first and only time the Laird signs: 'John Spottiswoode'. In addition to the above are various usual entries such as the other tenants or farm servants had against their names. Is John Paterson, then, someone special? As the Laird credits him with 'wages', he is not a tenant, and as Paterson's wage is only £3 per annum, he must be a farm servant. The only other explanation which seems feasible is that he had a farm of his own either on the estate or close by and rented it 'from the heirs of Mr. Veitch'. Apart from the usual items Paterson bought from the Laird, there is one which is especially interesting. It runs: 'To – stone unsmeared owl . . . 4/–'. As we have seen already, sheep and lambs were smeared with a mixture of tar and butter or oil. If a fleece was left unsmeared, its value was often higher. By contrast, a smeared fleece cost a buyer less – as in this case. So, owl is, apparently, wool.

Another interesting entry is 'By cloth cheeses £1. 9/–', which shows that cheese was made at Spottiswoode and that the cloths they needed were obtainable at that time. Paterson also bought the regulation 200 herring at 1s. 4d. But throughout the years he spent working at Spottiswoode he never drew any cash. Only when he left on 31st May, 1759 did he draw the arrears due.

The next man in the Diary is Alex Lindsay whom the Laird described as 'Servant and Herd Boy'. It seems a strange mixture of duties. It may also explain why he only remained at Spottiswoode for three years at the meagre rate of 15s. per annum. He was then dismissed and the Laird notes it as follows: 'N.B. There was a pair of shoes referred to myself for this last half year but he behaved so ill and was so backward in my absence and left his work at his pleasure that I would not give him em. He left my service at Martinmas 1758'.

Another farm servant whose name comes forward from Ledger C is James Crichton. For some reason, he has one page for items he bought from the Laird and the opposite page covers the work done and the rates charged. It would have been easier to read the Diary/Journal had this been the practice throughout. But it must be remembered that there were many illiterates at that time so that the Laird had to record transactions on their behalf. In those cases, a double-sided account was helpful.

James Crichton's work mainly centred round drainage and water 'failing', which is the work of cutting drains to float peat and brash down to the nearest water-course. He could also thresh corn (oats), but in Teviotdale measure, as the Laird records. There is little else of note under Crichton's name. But in 1757 the style of writing changes, although only for half a page. The spelling of Spottiswoode omits the 'e'. The Laird's handwriting resumes in June – after six months, with the use of a term not so far seen, viz. 'A forpit of good peas'. Crichton's wife also helps out regularly with whatever work is being done, namely, shearing at harvest and 'Gathering the snedings of the Firs'. That done, her husband makes some unusual purchases. He pays 9s. for two yards of black cloth and 1s. 6d. for two yards of 'shorge' (presumably, a coarse kind of serge). Next comes rather a mysterious entry: 'To his house rent . . . £1'. This is double the rate paid by James Rutherfoord and one or two others. But for work done at day wages, the Laird only allows Crichton the standard rate of 6d. per day. Does that, and what comes next, show the harder side of his character? 'By his Wife and Bairns gathering stones of ye clover s[outh] of ye house and at ye Hay . . . in all 3/10d. Ye Wife was allowed 4d. per day, ye old Daughter 3d. and ye young ones 2d.' They certainly had to work hard for their 3s. 10d. But was there perhaps a change of heart, because in 1758 Crichton's house-rent was reduced to 10s. like the rest.

There was also a change in the employment of Crichton's family. His wife gathered stones, as usual, but this time from a field called the Pikie Park – which still exists under that name. She was paid 4d. a day but the only daughter to help her was Mary who was paid 3d. a day though only for five days compared to her mother's eight. But in the same month, July, Crichton's wife worked the hay alone at 4d. and was then taken on for the harvest at 5d a day. This demonstrates the difference in value between the two.

In December 1760 there is a very unusual entry for Crichton: 'To two letters paid for him from his son . . . 2/6d'. In those days communication by letter was uncertain to say the least. Consequently, correspondence was spasmodic and addresses were often guessed at with doubtful accuracy. There were only 34 towns in the whole of Scotland where there was a postal point but the problem was how to find out if letters addressed to a particular individual were lying there. They were not delivered and could remain uncollected at the postal point for months. It would seem that Dod Mill on the Spottiswoode estate was, in fact, a postal point, possibly serving a large area of country around it. Supporting that view is an envelope in the Diary slit up the sides and opened out to make a sheet of paper. On one side is the Spottiswoode grain yield for 1779 and on the other the address: 'To John Spottiswoode of Spottiswoode, to be left at Dod's Mill'. The red mark of the sealing wax used by the sender is still to be seen.

As a result of such sluggish communication, news travelled fitfully and it could take weeks for reports of national events to arrive in distant places. According to Walker in his *History of the Hebrides*, 'Ministers of the Kirk supplicated for the King's long life weeks after his lamented Majesty had been buried and in the long specific prayers, many a time it was said "I thanked God for giving us a glorious victory when we had been shamefully beaten: for inspiring courage in the troops when they had run away; for success granted to our arms in battles that were never fought: for deliverance from plots that were never formed" '. Few, however, would match the charming frankness of the Highland minister of Alness, who, finding that his information had been erroneous, said from the pulpit: 'My brethren, it was a' lees I tellt ye last Sabbath!' (*Memoirs of a Highland Lady*).

However, there was one class of individual whose presence Scotland gladly did without – highwaymen! They stayed away, preferring the lush stamping grounds in which they operated so successfully south of the Border.

John Spottiswoode possibly found himself free also from another form of coercion which plagued his friends and relations in the south – the giving of 'vails'. These were presents given mainly to menservants and had the evil effect of holding down wages. If visiting a family of wealth or prominence, a guest would be expected to leave a guinea with the butler or manservant who brought his cloak and who might be better off than he. In the houses of the great, it was not uncommon (except in the country districts) for a guest to leave by passing along a file of footmen, giving each one as much as half a guinea and ending his evening much the poorer.

It was more common north of the Border to dole out 'drink money' or 'card money' or 'guest money'. It was an ancient practice in Scotland, the origin of which is unknown. The Laird did suffer from this pernicious practice and recorded it in his Diary. But the occasions on which he does so are very few.

Returning to the Diary entry concerning the two letters collected for John Crichton, each cost him 1s. 3d., a high price in those days. But where was Crichton's son? He could have enlisted in a Scottish regiment or gone to sea or taken himself off to the West Indies where rumour had it a man could quickly grow rich.

Around midsummer, Crichton and three others must have bought a bull between them because under 19th July, 1762 we have the following entry: 'To his 4th share of the Bull . . . £1. 3. 4d.'. That made the total cost £4 13s. 6d. However, the entry shows that these four shareholders had sufficient female cattle between them to justify buying a bull. But the Laird does not say whether he had a share in it or not. The fact that he financed it would suggest he had.

There are other entries against Crichton which contain a certain interest. For example, he ordered a pair of 'clog shoes, with carriage' for 2s. 4d. and bought a pound of snuff which cost 1s. 8d., and then sold the Laird a stack of oats. This would be quite a large one as it cost him £4 10s. He then put up a stake and rice dyke which is a hedge, tall enough to keep cattle in (or out) and made from cutting the bush or young hedge growth half way through, then bending it over and securing the leaning (or laid) branches by inserting vertical stakes every few yards to keep everything tight. This was not just hard work but skilful, requiring much practice. There is also mention of Crichton doing some 'failing of dykes'. This means topping off the last course of stone of a drystone dyke with turves cut for the purpose, either of heather, peat or sods. The idea was that the rain would run off these, away from the stones, keeping them dry. The next entry concerns drainage at Thornydyke march, an entry which fixes the position of the march.

At the end of 1762, Crichton was detailed for a job which none of the men would relish, namely pulling out stones from the moor and carting them away to make dykes. It would be a cold enough task on any winter's day, but working in the freezing cold in bare feet must have been very hard indeed, especially at the meagre rate of only 6d. per day. But this was normal for the time. Any laird who wanted to reclaim ground would have to remove the stones first and then dry up the cleaned ground with open ditches or stone-filled drains. It was a slow business but almost the only winter occupation available to a gang of men. The Laird would not want them standing idle with nothing to do (even when he did not have to pay them), and the men would not want to be idle either, as they earned nothing that way. But to carry out this task for a year, as Crichton did, must have been very trying. At least there was some variation in his next duty which was to build a 'fold dyke'. This was an earthen bank, usually built on one side of a ditch and using the spoil thrown out in its making. This was an early way of making an enclosure, with earthen dykes either on both sides of a ditch or just on one side. The next entry makes one wonder what Crichton planned by selling the Laird 30 threave of straw (720 sheaves). They cost him 10s. Crichton then bought a 'barrell' for 7d. It seems a strange price.

Far more interesting is the next entry: 'To half a rigg of turnipe . . . 2/−'. We do not know the length of that rig but Crichton must have considered its soil good enough to justify sowing turnips. Run-rigs, as they were known, were formed by ploughing the land into a crown, so that the middle furrows were the highest and thus the driest. The water would run off the lower furrows and be carried away. Rigs were ploughed out of the land all over Scotland from the Middle Ages until tile-drainage became commonplace in the nineteenth century. The theory was that the drier the land (the crown of the rig being the driest), the better the crop would be. Rigs can still be seen running uphill and on steep slopes throughout Scotland, such as along the Lammermuirs, in Midlothian and in many places throughout Roxburghshire. On the better class of farms, such as in East Lothian, Fife and Angus, tenants would draw lots each year for the best rigs, for middle-quality rigs and finally for the poorest. The length of these rigs varied but could be as much as 1,000 yards. Crichton's 'half rigg of turnipe' was probably not very long, perhaps 100 yards or so, as the rent of 2s. for the year was lower than a cow's grass. It is the fact of actually growing turnips in the field (not in the garden) which is intriguing, as 1762 was right at the start of the practice of growing turnips on a field scale in Scotland, for feeding to cattle and sheep.

Poor man or not, Crichton liked his pinch of snuff and regularly bought half a pound from the Laird. It cost him 8d. But he now had to care for another animal in addition to his milk cow and it cost him 10s. for the extra grazing. It was what the Laird termed a Quey and was almost certainly the progeny of Crichton's cow. 'Quey' is a term still used today, though 'heifer' is more common. Possibly, to meet his extra costs, Crichton must have persuaded his wife to take whatever work was offered in order to swell the family purse. Accordingly, she worked at the hay for 4d. per day, her usual rate, but she must have baulked at this wage for harvest work because she was awarded 6d. a day 'for shearing'. This was the term used for cutting down the grain crop using a sickle, which involved constant bending. Women shearers were not only better at it than men but usually cheaper. Crichton's daughter, Janet, was also taken on but only worked six and two thirds days according to the Laird, although he had to pay her the same wage as her mother. Their daughter Jean also did some shearing but only for three days at a lump sum of 1s. 9d. Meantime, Crichton himself was engaged 'In throwing out 106 roods of ditch at the Mill park'. This looks like a double fold on the top of which thorns might well have been planted to form enclosures. The Mill Park is still to be seen. It was Crichton's last work at Spottiswoode.

The Laird noted in his Diary: 'Crichton was a Lothian man and came from the Parish of Ratho. Mr. Pater of Chapel brought him to this Country He began to work to me in Spring of 1747, his first work was the sunk fence of the Long Walk. His family came in the 1748 and he dug stones in ye Pikie Park and in ye be-east ye Lawn and wrought every oyr [other] kind of work, his eldest son, James, was sometime my herd and drove my plow [plough] in ye 1753. he served ye Masons as a barrowman but he and some of ye Masons, commiting some trespass in ye Garden, I turned him off on which he went into Northumberland and wroght labouring work for sometime and then went to sea, made some money and came home in January 1764 and persuaded his father to settle with his family at Alnwick where he is gone this Novmbr 1764'. Crichton seems to have done his best to expand his small capital and had worked at all the jobs he was given at Spottiswoode. He was there for over 30 years.

William Turnbull was the last man to come from the missing Ledger C. In 1752 his daughter died and he had to ask the Laird to pay the funeral expenses for him, amounting to £3 14s. 2d. They were paid back promptly. For the first time, 'multure meal' is mentioned in the Journal, Turnbull having to pay 13s. 9d. to cover 11 stone he had bought. He was the tenant of a small farm on the estate, his rental of both house and farm amounting to £1 6s. 8d. He also rented a plot of land in the orchard for 10s. He was employed by the Laird more as a gardener than a general farm servant, although his wages were on a similar level to theirs. The Laird recorded: 'By his working the Walk down from ye big gate ye foot walk and yett down from ye Rowing Trees'. John Spottiswoode spelt words with absolute freedom. There were no rules, as 'Rowing' trees shows. Turnbull was another of the men who bought 200 herring at a time from the Laird and he paid the same as them – 8d. per 100. There is nothing very noteworthy about Turnbull. He knew what he had to do and did it. One small entry concerns the leg of a stot. He paid the Laird 5s. for it. A stot is a grown bullock and may have been wanted by Turnbull for salting down for the winter. Later that year (1760) he buys the leg of a dead sheep and receives his wages of £5 yearly. At the end of 1762 he buys a fat ewe for 5s. 6d. and 'another ewe not good' for 1s. 6d. But he liked his little extravagances and bought through the Laird shoes at Lauder for 10s. 6d. Six months later he bought more shoes from Romanis, the Lauder cobbler, costing 4s. 6d. Three years later they cost 9s. In 1769 he paid Romanis a further 9s. Although the Laird does not say so, it appears from what he writes next that William Turnbull died because the following appears at the end of his account: 'To cash to John Young as Heir to Wm and Jo. Wauch's paid thus by timber from ye Flas wood 24/– to his son Sandy – To his son James in cash 20/– and sent him in cash by the Schoolmaster Saturday 13 January 1770 12/– inde [thus] £2. 16/–'. Although no balance is officially struck, Turnbull's account is apparently cleared by this payment.

The last to mention of the men who were established at Spottiswoode when the Diary/Journal was begun is James Watson. He was not a farm servant but 'A Gardiner at Dunse', as the Laird described him. But his family were not against doing ordinary farm work, when there was no specialised gardening to do, as they were paid comparatively high rates. The account opens accordingly: 'By Thirty Two days of his son Valentine at 6d. per diem with his meal . . . 16/3d.'. Normally, the Laird did not include meal, as this was an extra cost to him and a bounty to the man.

Watson is given a double page in the Journal – the left-hand side of the ledger covers services performed by him (or his son) and the other side (the credit side) is for articles supplied by Spottiswoode. The rate at which James Watson was paid was quickly established – 'By 32 days of himself at 1/– per diem with his meal'. In other words twice what the Spottiswoode men received. The reason is obvious. Gardeners were few and any there were had to be remunerated according to the market.

Watson's first task was to plan out the grounds at Spottiswoode and then 'stake out the divisions and strips' which the Laird wanted to plant. This alone cost 3s. After that initial entry comes a whole list of days worked by Watson, namely, six days, seven days, two days, one day and so on, but nowhere does the Journal detail what work was done. For three years, Watson's account is made up of isolated days without detail of what he did. Only when the Laird starts to order seed is there a change. Thus we have: 'By 5 firlots of bran' followed by '2 garden Siths' costing 3s. 6d. for the pair, followed by 26 'libb' of pease at 2d. per lb; 4lb red clover at 5d. per lb; 2oz turnip and 1ooz radish for 4d.; 5lb red clover; and also field turnip. Most of these seeds would be for the garden but not the red clover. This amount of seed would cover two thirds of an acre and was therefore being grown on a field scale, probably for feeding cattle and then cleaning up with sheep. Next comes an intriguing entry: 'To the Bell and Custom for the butter at Duns . . . 4d.'. These men used to go round the streets ringing a bell to advertise the arrival in the town of meat or butter or whatever a producer had for sale – in this case, salt butter. A small fee was charged. After this flurry, Watson reverted to day wages and from that time on hardly sold the Laird anything. The exceptions were: 'Two syth stones', i.e. sharpening stones, for 10d. and 1lb whin seed. In those days whins were grown to feed cattle in winter which were often four years old before being sold at the Falkirk and Crieff Trysts. If his animals died from starvation, a man would have no money to pay the rent or buy meal to feed his family. Whins were a colourful if prickly crop but, if treated properly, they answered their purpose.

To prepare them, some kind of implement was needed to crush the shoots, and eventually one Baillie Young of Perth set up a mill in 1778 which did this. Others used a big round or conical stone up to four feet high, and before long many farms had some form of crusher. It is worthy of note that John Spottiswoode was growing whins, presumably to feed his cattle, 20 years before Baillie Young set up his crusher. The procedure was to pick the young shoots of whin (though young shoots of Scots Fir served just as well), then lay them in the path of the big stone, which was pulled in a circle by a horse or bullock. An acre of whins could provide keep for six horses over four months. In cases where a man was unable to set up a crusher, the whins would be beaten with a flail or boiled to soften them. The use of whin, or furze, meant that far fewer cattle died in winter and bigger numbers went to the Trysts.

The relationship between the Laird and James Watson lasted from 1753 to 1761. There is little other information about what Watson did at Spottiswoode during his various visits, but he seems to have supervised the growing of vegetables and fruit and helped to establish the young trees which we know John Spottiswoode was always anxious to plant. But by far the most interesting entries in the Diary under Watson's name concern the sale to the Laird of six silver teaspoons.

The transaction was carried out in two stages. On 29th November, 1755, Watson received a part payment of 10s. 6d., and on July 3rd 1756 he received the balance of 16s. 8d. On the same day, John Spottiswoode bought from Watson several other items, as follows: one and a half pounds of green tea with a canister for 7s. 6d.; one pound of chocolate for 5s.; also for mending a watch, he paid 1s. 6d.

These are unusual items, especially the six silver teaspoons. So how did a gardener come across them and how could he afford to sell them at well under 30s.? We can only guess, but Duns at that time was a well-known spa, relying very much on well-to-do visitors coming from the north of England 'to take the waters' and stay for a few days. They would bring their servants with them and, of course, their Green and Bohea tea in order to entertain their friends. When their visit drew to an end, their servants would be ordered to pack up their effects and next day they would set off home. Many would spend the night at an English inn (which were numerous and well appointed), so that it might be several days before they found they had been robbed. Was this, perhaps, how James Watson came by the six silver spoons? Be that as it may, the Laird balanced his account and on 11th May, 1764 paid Watson what was owing – 15s. His name does not appear again.

13

The Laird and his Men (II)

JOHN SPOTTISWOODE was always anxious to employ masons as they alone had the skills which were needed on such an estate. After the Aitchison family came two men in partnership – James Nisbet and John Winter. Their duties covered all kinds of masonry needs, such as making and hanging gates (the Laird calls them yetts or sometimes yeats). They also had the job of mending drystone dykes and building others. From what the Laird writes they appear as reliable and able men. One of the tasks he gave them was 'Seven days at ye mill trows'. This meant seven days making and laying a wooden spout into the mill, presumably from a spring or burn higher up. For this, they received 8d. a day 'with meat'. In other words, the Laird supplied their food. They had arrived at Spottiswoode in 1755 as a team and they continued to work that way until 1764 when for no stated reason they left. But not before John Winter had bought one stone of wool and Nisbet two stones and one fleece of English wool which weighed 5lbs. This is in contrast to Scottish fleeces which were more or less destroyed by smearing and suffered from the senseless way lambs were reared, ensuring small and stunted animals. Their fleeces weighed only 1 to 1½ lbs. Nisbet and Winter left on 26th December.

Robert Jamieson arrived two years after Nisbet and Winter and was put to general farm work at the usual rate of 6d. a day. The Diary says little about him, the Laird remaining silent when a man does what he is told without complaint. However, John Spottiswoode bought a 'syth' from him at a cost of 2s. 6d. and Jamieson bought a 'parcell of hay' for 4s. It is the first time the Laird sells hay by the parcel. In 1758 Jamieson left but no reason is given.

In 1759 Robert Welsh came and went. He was engaged as the Master's servant but left after a year. Robert Thin 'paid him his wages at Pask Fair in Lauder being £3 13. 6d.'. Pask or Pash Fair was Easter, or Paschal, Day Fair.

The Laird kept looking for another mason because of the growing number of houses and dykes he was building. He found one in Thomas Grieve and paid him 1s. a day laying paving stones (the Laird calls them casaways), mending dykes and building others, so the work of making enclosures went on apace. But it would seem that Grieve had ground of his own within the estate because he sold the Laird 'a pleugh' for 7s., either because he had bought a more modern one or because he could secure another one at a cheaper price. Grieve was able to hire out his man to John Spottiswoode at 6d. a day for three days before selling him 'a new beam and head and sheth to ye little plow', all for 4s. A sheth is a stick with which a mower whets his scythe. It would seem from what John Spottiswoode then wanted that Thomas Grieve was both a carpenter and a mason, because he sold him a 'cartfull of timber in ye Flas Wood for 3/−' and then bought from him 'a beam for another plow — not come home yet' for 2s. 6d. But the Laird must have been pleased with what Grieve made as he ordered from him two more ploughs. This was too early to be one of the new James Small ploughs which would soon be introduced. These would be much lighter than the ancient Scots plough which was in everyday use and which required several horses or oxen to pull it and two or three men to drive it, with a 'gad-boy' whipping up the team. Small's plough would work with one horse, or at the most, a pair of horse and one man. Grieve was next given the job of 'making and furnishing wood to a Cart Wheel' and was paid 12s. 6d. for it. Next he made a cheese-press and again hired out his man to the Laird. But he must have been pleased with the next task the Laird gave him: 'for the Body of a lime cart and axle tree and Trams with a pair of Trams for ye 4-wheeled chaise'. This was in 1768 when carriages and wheeled vehicles were still few and many carts were built with solid wooden wheels which warped and broke by rough usage on the dreadful tracks. John Spottiswoode must have been one of the few in the county who owned his own carriages.

The old Scots plough, used by everyone from the Highlands to the Tweed, was made largely of wood with only the odd metal part. It was difficult and cumbersome to work and if it ploughed an acre a day without breaking down it was doing well. John Spottiswoode was clearly using several old-style ploughs at this time, which is why Thomas Grieve needed wood from Flass. The ploughs would require frequent repair and Grieve was constantly being asked to provide new ones. At 7s. each, they were not dear. But suddenly, he is taken off working in wood to labour for three days quarrying stones, followed by two days working with his son 'putting up the Sclaters' Scaffolds'. That done, he was put to mending the slaps (gaps) in the Easter Park before going back to working timber. He drew two cart loads from Flass and was then set to work on the Hablon Houses 'possessed by the Minister'. Then comes a matter of considerable concern to the Laird. He wanted Grieve and his son to be 'Taking down and putting up the gabel of the kitchen vent which I was obliged to take down that year [1769] for its smoking so intolerably that it was spoiling the whole furniture in the house – gave 'em their diet and paid in cash – £1. 5. 7d.'.

That done, Grieve and his son took down and re-erected the vents at the Mason's Lodge. And then something entirely different. He was told to mend 'The Chinese rail, west of the Lady's Walk'. Although this suggests that Mistress Spottiswoode used this Walk, it is the first time she is referred to, however obliquely.

By this time, Grieve is fully established as a mason/carpenter, and judging from the variety of tasks he is given his work satisfied John Spottiswoode. Accordingly, Grieve's son and also his apprentice are taken on, the former at the excellent wage of 10d. and the latter at 8d. This is a clear indication that the national economy was improving. Further evidence supports this view. The Laird wants some thatching done at 'William Bower's house' and has to raise his rates to 14d. a day to Thomas Grieve and the same to his son, with the apprentice drawing 11d. It does not follow that these two young men would receive this money in their hands because Thomas Grieve controlled the whole operation and decided how much each youngster would receive. That was the system.

The next work they were asked to do was 'building the new Offices', which on the evidence is likely to refer to the great stable yard, with its groom's house, open sheds, stables and coach-house, which fortunately still stands. By this time, the Grieve family had really steady work, covering several months. But eventually it was finished and they reverted to more mundane tasks such as 'ringing a pair of cart-wheels'. Then suddenly the Grieve family leave, their time at Spottiswoode at an end. The Laird obviously felt some generosity towards them: 'December, 1781. Gave him a note of this ballance and in regard it has been long owing, (£17. 18. 8d.) it was made up to £20 sterling therefore the same is discharged, day and date as above'. The Diary is then signed by Thomas Grieve. It is a neat signature.

Robert Thin did not last long. The Laird notes down the terms of his employment: 'He entered as a Servant within the House Martinmas 1758 at £2 sterling in ye half year. I agreed with him to take the charge of all ye work and men at Whitsun 1759 for which I was to give him a free House, 1 Cow's grass summer and winter and fodder. 6 bolls meal for his meat and £4 sterling in money'. Although the Diary does not say so, these were the terms for a full year's work. There is nothing stated in the Diary other than the payments he received and the goods he was given – all in accordance with the above terms. In May 1762 Thin sold the Laird 'a red Quey calf for £1', which was a bargain.

After that his wife, Maggie Brown, was engaged to shear the harvest which she did for '14 and two third days at 5d a day'. She then worked at the hay at 4d. a day while he borrowed against his wages to hire a boar to serve two swine for 2s. This was a service fee. A further 2s. was given to the maltman at Lauder. Then in the margin is a tiny little note: 'His wife dyed 9th April, 1764'. Thin left Spottiswoode in June 1765.

George Peacock arrived in June of 1760 but there was nothing special about him. He was given the usual tasks. But he did buy from the Laird a firlot of potatoes for 2s. and half a firlot of beans at 10s. the boll. From this we can assume that he wanted some variety in his diet. There is also some variety in the Laird's spelling, for he writes: 'To a years rent of his house aiker', meaning acre. Peacock is noted as having worked at 'ye muir at ye foot of ye lawn'. This shows that the house gardens and grounds were still indeed surrounded by 'muir'. Peacock is given '2 baxes to construct near his house'. These would be to carry away drain water. Baxes are usually box-type drains, i.e. built with four square slabs, then covered with soil. They were ideal where water levels were likely to rise rapidly after heavy rain. Peacock must have owned some cows because the Laird notes his quarter share of the bull as £1 3s. 4d. He also rents him '2 riggs of turnips' for 7s. 6d. This indicates the presence of cattle but not of sheep, no ground having been let to Peacock by the Laird for 'grassing sheep' as he terms it. But in May of 1764 he moves to another house 'And is to possess it with ye ground within ye ditches . . . and Thornydyke march . . . for 3 years, the first two he is to pay £2 10/– and ye last £3. sterling, ye rent payable at Candlemas and Lammas'.

It would appear from this and other similar entries that as John Spottiswoode cleared and reclaimed land, he let it to tenants. By doing this he extended the arable acreage and increased his rentals and therefore his capital. Lord Kames of Blair Drummond and his son Henry were the great exponents of this. In clearing peat from the great Moss of Kincardine, nine feet deep, Kames exposed a fertile clay which grew excellent cereal crops and grass. When the work was finished, Henry found he had 300 more farms in his possession. But he did not charge excessive rents, preferring to see his new tenants establish themselves and place themselves in a position to pay rents. In the same way, Peacock was left to work his farm and to use his slack times to do ditching for the Laird. In order to decide how much these ditches were to cost, the schoolmaster, James Nisbet, was engaged to do the measuring. But Peacock also had hay to cut for the Laird. In the summer of 1764 he 'cut the hay in the Third and Teind Parks being 13 acre 10 perches English at 1/6 per acre'. This was a big job for which he earned less than £1.

Next comes the first real clue to the amount of turnip the Laird grew. In May 1764, Peacock was 'at the Turnipe for 32 days at 8d. a day'. This can only mean sowing or singling at that time of year. It also indicates beyond doubt that John Spottiswoode was an early grower of turnips to feed animals. Then comes an old word which the Laird does not use often, i.e. 'Mailing'. This is a rented farm.

There was now a turnpike road running through some of the Spottis-woode land and Peacock was given the job of cleaning out the sunk fence beside it. The laying down of these roads, following an Act of Parliament in 1751, marked the beginning of the economic revolution which swept through Scotland at this time. Instead of the proprietors having to maintain the roads which went through their land by supplying men and tools, the local authority took over the responsibility. The state, through Parliament, laid down what roads were to come under public jurisdiction and a collection of maps was published under the title *Taylor & Skinner's Survey and Maps of the Roads of North Britain or Scotland, published for the Authors as the Act directs, the 20th March, 1776*. They were also called The Great Roads, so they did not include side roads or lesser roads. Instead of goods being conveyed on the backs of pack animals, which were mainly poor brutes of small strength and little size, wheeled carts came slowly into common use, conveying goods at a tenth of the cost and in a tenth of the former time. Instead of proprietors having to supply men and tools to repair the tracks on certain days of the year, they were assessed in equal proportion and this money eventually went to the laying down of service-able roads which were properly maintained. But this all took time and on the estates and farms progress was slow as always where change affected the land.

Peacock became responsible for the cutting, stacking and driving of peat at Spottiswoode. We know from the Diary that there was 'A peat road' up which supplies of peat for the winter were driven. But Peacock was also given instructions on every other aspect of peat usage. He was to 'cast', i.e. cut, the peats into regular slices, and then make 21 stacks of it, each stack to be 12ft long and 6ft broad and 20 peats high. For this he was paid 3s. 6d. per stack. That done, he was set to planting 'Half a hundred Spruce Firs in ye Pikie Park strip' for 6d., and following that he was set to sliping (planting) with H. Foreman 3,100 firs at 18s. per thousand in Paddowhill Park, Peacock's share being 2s. 3d. That done, he was asked to 'cast' 15,500 divots for the mill houses for which he received a mere 15s. 6d. These seem low rates, although possibly the going rates, but the Laird may have driven too hard a bargain. Peacock left and John Spottiswoode writes of him in 1770: 'He has wrought with me since summer 1760 till July last that he went off my work for greed of a job in mowing hay at Thornydyke and as he was making money had got up his Family pretty well and living comfortably upon the encouragement I gave him. I was so exasperate at him, judging nothing could content him that I turned him off and cleared him to this day'. (The balance he received was £4 10s. 10d.) The last job he did for John Spottiswoode was 'By 4 days thatching the smidding [sic] and the Sitt House at the Mill at 6d. per day . . . 2/–'. One can understand Peacock's resentment, which would be aggravated by being paid at the very lowest rates.

William Urie and John Thynne, Masons, entered the Laird's service in April, 1760. He must have been a relieved man as there was much work awaiting skilled masons. Accordingly, it is no surprise to see the Laird drawing up a signed contract and taking notes of all these two men did. Thus we have, right at the beginning: 'By the Easter Park belonging to ye East Farm and in my hand this Whitsun 63 chain 32 Links equal to 206 Rood . . . £12 17. 6d.'. By the finish they had built 382 roods and 3 links. In distance, this amounted to 2,674 yards and it took until 29th December 1761 to complete. But John Spottiswoode would have been well pleased as he makes no criticism and no comment. However, he does check the work by having a Mr. W. Walker measure the dykes. Is this the minister perhaps? This completed the contract with William Urie and John Thynne who had earned between them £23 17s. 6d. It does not look much, but in those days a year's wage in money was between £5 and £6 at day rates.

As far as attracting skilled labour to Spottiswoode was concerned, the Laird was fortunate in that the main road south to Newcastle passed right in front of the estate's gates. Travellers making for England, where working conditions and wages were better, might well stop at Spottiswoode looking for a meal and shelter for the night. A good inn was a great rarity in Scotland at this time, so travellers tended to seek food and shelter in private houses. Naturally, the conversation would turn to what was happening on the estate and what the wages were. If they matched what the visitor wanted, he might well decide to take a job there and seek an interview. If he was in any way skilled, the Laird would be likely to try and persuade him to stay. Such an applicant might well have been John Ker who claimed to be a gardener and ditcher – just the skills which were needed at Spottiswoode.

However, the Laird clearly decided to be cautious, setting Ker to ditching for the first three months. Then in October, he was told to lift potatoes for five days which is proof that these were grown on a field scale. Only when Ker showed that at least he was genuine where ditching was concerned was he given some gardening to do. But first, he was given two other men to assist him at the horse pond, he being paid 1s. a day and they 8d. He and another man were then transferred to the bleaching field, possibly to see how they did there. The Laird does not say what was needed in the bleach field, but as timber uprights supported the ropes which carried the flax, to let the weather bleach it, the weight would pull them down. Most country people at this time grew a little flax which the women folk would scutch, then spin and finally weave into coarse clothing. Flax was a durable fibre which thrived out of doors, where the rain would continually wet it. The climate on the east coast and in parts of the Border country was ideal for growing flax, and by the middle years of the eighteenth century, flax spinning and weaving was a thriving industry. It is understandable, therefore, that John Spottiswoode would want his 'bleaching-field' to be in good order. The Diary also speaks of lintseed, i.e. the seed of the flax plant which would be used for growing flax or crushed for its oil. John Ker was slowly introduced to the gardening needs of the estate, presumably because he had proved his abilities. First he was told 'To cut 18 Rood of the Hornbeam hedge and then to cut the birch hedge in the Long Walk at a penny a Rood'. And then for a reason he does not explain, the Laird orders Ker to cut down 40 lime trees in the back court.

After that, it was back to the drains! Ker was paid only 1s. 8d. for cutting the limes, so it cannot have been a long job. From what is said later, it seems these lime trees were hedges and 'cutting' meant trimming. In August 1758, Ker was ordered to work with Mr. Watson for 8d. a day, with three men. It is the first and only time that James Watson of Duns is mentioned as working with any of the Spottiswoode men. This could explain why it took so long before the Laird gave Ker work in the gardens or grounds of Spottiswoode. In 1759 he did so, however, and had Ker 'tending the Borders in the Walks and flower plots below the East Pavilion'. He was also asked to sow 'ye grass seed', but it was not long before he was back digging drains and ditches. Then, for a change, he was told to weed the potatoes and then work 'One day at the Tulips'. This being in October, he must have been planting bulbs.

The Laird now speaks of hiring Ker's man, which means Ker is a tenant of a small farm. But he seems well enough set up because he buys from John Spottiswoode 59lbs of English wool and then a further 56lbs. These two purchases cost him £2 16s., but as the Laird owed him more than this, they cost him nothing in actual cash. In October 1765 he left. But three years later he returned. As the Laird laconically puts it: 'He entered to work in the plantings as below'. It was an impressive programme. First, there were hedges to cut and clean in various parts and after that the biggest project the estate had so far seen – the planting of young trees. John Spottiswoode had purchased some of them in London but the Diary does not tell us exactly where. All it does is give a list of the numbers and kinds of trees planted, which were as follows:

1,200 Scots Firs	100 Spruce Firs
900 Oaks	1,300 Beech – part whereof pited.
4,400 Elms all pited	
4,000 Thorns	
18,000 Seedling Firs, sliped (planted).	

The total cost of planting was just over £12.

In addition to the saplings, the Laird also bought a quantity of beech mast and acorns in London which he planted in his own nursery at Thimblehall. Apart from them, the Spottiswoode men had planted 30,000 young trees. As this took time, the Laird had to arrange the men's lodging.

He tells us that James Allan and James Cribbis put them up and the cost of doing so amounted to £4 10s. 7d. Although the Diary does not say so, Ker was possibly in charge of the planting and must have satisfied the Laird. But he was not happy with the cost because he adds this warning: 'Nota. This too dear. I enquired at W. Shiels anent ye prices of planting and he said when they made the pits 1s. per 100 and when slipt [planted] 18d. per 1,000. By both these I found they made above 18d. per day'. If this was correct, the men were being paid three times the usual rate for farm work.

There follows a special entry for John Ker: 'By sneding and cleaning the whole planting – £3'. This must have referred to other woods and plantations which had been planted some time before. The 30,000 seedlings above would have been, as yet, too small to sned.

John Ker left the following year (1769) but the Laird made out that he still owed him 'For 24 libb English wool at 1/– per libb . . . £1. 4/–'.

Two men had meantime come and gone – George Hyslop who entered as servant to the Laird in 1755, and John Fairbairn who came to Bruntaburn Mill three years later. The only interesting items are Hyslop's wage of £4 per year and a pair of shoes valued at 3s. However, part of his duty was to look after the chaise and see that it was properly oiled. The Laird charged him 8d. for the oil! He also had him pay 1s. 7d. for candles for the stable. It seems strange that Hyslop should have to pay for looking after his employer's goods. However, Hyslop left at the May Term (28th) 1758 'And went to serve the Minister, Mr. Scot'. But not having received his free pair of shoes that year, he was given the value of them (3s.) in cash. This was the general rule all over the south of Scotland, viz. that a man agreed a money wage with his employer and a money value for items such as shoes, a house, grassing for a cow, meal, bere, malt etc. If he did not receive one or all of these, he received a cash payment instead.

John Fairbairn was a miller and arrived to operate the Bruntaburn Mill. When not doing that, he was given labouring jobs about the place. The Laird debits him with 1s. 4d., for '200 Heron', which is the ruling price at the time, but it is strange to see the Laird's spelling slip, when all along he has spelt 'Herring' correctly. Fairbairn left in 1758, only a month or two after coming to Spottiswoode. No explanation or reason is given by the Laird. He was succeeded by John Neil who was also a miller and who arrived in 1758. He worked on the estate at the usual 6d. per day – presumably when he had no milling to do – and so did his wife and daughter, Mary. There is a reference to Mary as follows: 'By 1 pair of shoes to his daughter Mary when she left my family at Whitsun, 1761'. Was she a servant in the house, looking after children perhaps? It would seem so, judging from the words used about her leaving the Laird's family. But she came back, as we shall see. There is an unusual entry under Neil's name in February, 1762: 'By his Son John's fee as goadman in winter 60 for ye year – 18/4d'. As always, this was credited to the father and not to John. The use of 'goadman' is interesting. A 'goadman' was one who walked beside the ploughing team of three or four horses and perhaps three or four oxen as well as two to three men, all engaged in tugging the old single-furrow Scots plough, often uphill. The goadman goaded the animals to keep them moving. This task was usually given to a youth or a young boy.

When James Small brought out his revolutionary swing-plough in 1767, the whole farming scene began to change. Instead of all those animals, weak from lack of feeding, Small's plough needed one or two horses and no oxen. But the biggest saving in cost was in the manning of it, as only one ploughman was needed. It would be surprising if John Spottiswoode did not learn of Small's invention quite early on because Small was farming at Blackadder Mount in 1763 and was making his experiments there. News of these would be certain to spread through the whole of the Borders and the men at Spottiswoode would hear of them early on. Blackadder Mount was not far across the hill. John Neil left in January that year.

Thomas Shortridge arrived at Spottiswoode in June 1761, and the first job he had was 'Thrashing Crichton's Oats, bought by me'. That done, he did ordinary farm work at 6d. a day. But he must have had a small farm with cattle of his own, being the third man in the deal which purchased the bull, his quarter share being the same as the others, £1 3s. 4d. But he did not survive long, falling sick while mowing the lawn, from which illness he never recovered.

James Cribbis 'Entered as a House Labouring Servant' at Whitsun 1761. His wage was agreed as £4 15s. per year, and once again the Laird specifies that this is Sterling. Although the Union of Parliaments took place in 1707 and all Scottish coin had been called in to change into Sterling, it was necessary for a man to state clearly whether he was negotiating in pounds Scots or pounds Sterling. The reason was that it took £12 Scots to equal £1 Sterling. John Spottiswoode now introduces another *Nota*: 'At Whitsun, 1762 I gave him the charge of ye work in place of Ro. Thynne and the above wage with the addition of the 10 sheeps grass in the Flas over and above ye said wage to make him take the more care'. There are several points here. Did a 'House Labouring Servant' mean that he had quarters in the Big House or was his place of work the Big House? At this time, unmarried men usually took their meals in the main house. Segregation of farm cottages from the big house of the farmer was still to come. At this time, therefore, only married farm servants had a house for their family, as did tenant farmers.

Cribbis was a single man as it turned out. The Laird adds another *Nota* to what he has already written: 'At Whitsun last, 1764 he married one of the maids in ye House & in regard of his going to his own house I gave him just Ro. Thinn's wages, viz, meal, cow's grass, House & £4 wages' (per annum).

The years passed and Cribbis apparently did his work, without complaints being recorded by the Laird. He and his wife were asked by John Spottiswoode if they would board a gardener called John Moffat from November 1765 to November 1766 at 20d. per week, which they did and were paid £4 6s. 8d. In regard to grazing ten sheep in the Flas Wood, this would be where the Haigs had laid out a drystone dyke, to protect the other sections of timber from damage by grazing animals. At the same time, it was good management to have either sheep or cattle to clean up and manure the section felled in preparation for new planting, and this is exactly what the Laird did. In October, 1768 Cribbis bought two ewes from John Spottiswoode for 9s. 4d. and then sold him his milk cow (for which he had grassing as part of his wage). On the surface this looks very unwise. But several possibilities arise for his doing this. Either the cow was breaking out and wandering off, which is quite likely because one acre for grazing was not enough at that time, or she could not hold a calf or failed to provide enough milk. If any of these was the reason, Cribbis was right to dispose of his cow and instead run a few lambs. The Laird appears to have been glad of the opportunity to buy the Cribbis cow and did so for £8. This was two years' wages for Cribbis and must have delighted him. After ten years in John Spottiswoode's employ, he was owed £21 6s., which was a happy position to be in. It meant that he was able to save a little money year by year. But was he giving satisfaction to the Laird? Let us leave it to him to tell us: '1st March, 1774. He had been about 10 years with me but I always thought him very indifferently qualified for the charge he had and he turned so wretchedly greedy that I was at last obliged to Turn him off in June 1771 for his bad practices to say no worse of him'.

John Prophet came to Spottiswoode in 1762 and 'Entered as a Household servant to drive the Chaise, take care of the horses and work at every kind of work and came in place of Jas Wilson. Wages 1 cow's grass in ye parks and fodder, a free house and £5 sterling', i.e. for the year. But on 30th May 1765 he left. The Laird was intent on his signing a receipt for the balance of what he was owed and giving details of what outlays he had had, viz. 'To Turnpike and a Horse shoe . . . 1/9d. He made a demand for some working clothes so I gave him a £5 note in full'.

William Redpath came as a labourer in 1767 and was taken on 'To form the Road in the west avenue at 1/6 per rood being 21 foot to the roof, which is ye road rood'. When finished, it measured out at 58 roods which at 21 feet to the rood is 406 yards. But with his usual deep attention to detail, the Laird comments: 'There was 5 roods that would not form for ye hollowness of ye ground and therefore was laid with stones and it was only formed as far west as the old Firs are planted'. Redpath was then given some tree planting to do and put in 1,500 firs. He left on eighteenth May 1771 which, as the Laird tells us, was a Saturday.

Thomas Jamieson had come to work at Spottiswoode in 1762, entering as a labouring servant. He was given a free house, cow's grass and fodder, six bolls of meal and £3 10s. sterling. He was the fourth shareholder of the bull and paid his share of £1 3s. 4d. Apart from taking a half rig of turnip, he did not attract any other comment from the Laird who said this of him: 'Nota. He left my service at Whitsun 1764. He was a very good natured, honest Servant so far as I could ever discover for the years he served me. He dyed of a fever in harvest 1770 and left a widdow and young children very poor'.

Andrew Cribbis began to work at Spottiswoode in April 1763. He was a mason 'and arrived when I was at London'. This was the visit to the metropolis recorded by James Boswell (see Introduction). Then for some reason best known to himself the Laird records the financial arrangement with Cribbis in both Sterling and Merks Scots, viz. '1s. 1d. and one third of a penny per day, or 1 mark Scots'. Cribbis mended some drystane dykes and then spent thirteen days building pillars for park gates. Next, he spent the same number of days 'At the Sithouse at Paddowhall'. This was a barn or a cowhouse and sometimes a dwelling. Paddock or Paddie Hall became the site of the home farm and cottages, but it is unlikely that any of the surviving buildings are as early as this.

Cribbis could not complain at the lack of variety in the work he was given. He laid sivers at the sides of 'Ye formed roads' and helped put up gates 'East of ye dove-coat at 1 mk.' and built 28 roods of the semi-circle at Hardacres at 1s. 2d. per rood. Could Cribbis only calculate in Scots merks? Almost all the cash entries against his name are made in this currency. The semi-circle the Laird mentions is still visible. But there was so much work wanting to be done, mainly in establishing new stone dykes or mending others that Cribbis was authorised to bring two more masons to Spottiswoode. The Laird records this, as follows: 'Andrew Cribbis in May '68 brought Robert and John Sheills, Masons, to work dry stone dykes and they have all three worked in company almost ever since but as their work was always paid and some of it, viz, the Great Circle not finished till lately, I never booked what money they got till now'. He goes on to record all the dykes built and mended with a special mention of 'Building the "smiddy" at Thimblehall' and 'The face dyke north side of the road, viz, that side next to the Mill land, west to the road that goes to ye Mill'. A face dyke is a wall of stone on one side and earth or turf on the other. Trees were sometimes planted on top to bind the wall. Such walls are still seen all over the former Spottiswoode lands, though often in ruinous condition. Cribbis and the Sheills brothers were now a team, working together, but they must have complained about their rate of pay because the Laird writes: 'These last at 8d. [per rood] which being thought too small a price, I was obliged to raise ye rest to 9d.'.

There was still a great deal for masons to do. They had the sitthouse to repair and 'Two Cott houses' (usually cottages for married farm servants) as well as 'Re-building the byre and stable at ye mill and taking down and rebuilding the Kiln'. This was used for drying the grain so that it did not heat in winter and become wasted. Next of interest was 'By building the Great Circle on the top of Brotherfield Muir finished only in May 1770, being 115 roods at 15d per rood'. This is important information because a later proprietor of Spottiswoode, Alicia Anne, who married the younger brother of the Duke of Buccleuch, had the Great Circle explored, believing it to be a Pictish fort. Nothing was found in the way of weapons or artifacts, and no member of the family apparently knew of the existence of the Diary or its record of the building of the circle. The money paid out by Alicia Anne in her search would be far greater than the £7 4s. spent on building it.

Andrew Cribbis and the Sheills brothers must have persuaded the Laird to let them build their own house because he agreed to this and paid them the cost: £8 6s. As so often seemed to happen, just when a man appeared to be settled, something occurred to unsettle him. The Laird tells the story: 'Nota: The house on the road east of Pyetshaw was built purposely for 'em as they had entered into contract with me anent the building & leading the stones to all my dykes. The house was no sooner built in '70 and possessed when John Sheil's wife and Andrew Cribbis could not agree so Shiel left it in '71, lived all summer in Rockieknold and went with his wife to Borland from whence I brought them and lamed a good horse which never recovered. The two Brothers wrought by themselves at dry stone dykes but in building houses, Andrew Cribbis wrought with 'em'. Robert and John Shiells now had 'a prentice' to whom the Laird paid 6d. per day. Not so many years before, all the men at Spottiswoode were paid only 6d., so the inevitable inflation which followed general prosperity was already setting in.

In order to erect all the dykes at Spottiswoode (there must have been miles of them) stone had to be found, over and above the stones prised out of the moor. The Laird certainly had access to a quarry, but whether he owned it, one cannot say. Probably he did. Traces of several small quarries survive on the estate. At any rate, the Shiells brothers quarried 79 roods in 1770 and were paid 8d. a rood. By this time, they were owed over £40, half of which the Laird paid in October, 1773. They also bought a quey from him and paid him £4 12s. 6d., at which time Robert Shiell left. John Spottiswoode does not give the reason. John Shiell and the 'prentice' worked on, but all three had left by the end of 1773. The Laird does not give a reason but it seems more than likely they would find other work as there were opportunities opening up all over the county.

Andrew Cribbis continued at Spottiswoode, however. He bought a Highland cow from the Laird and thus showed his knowledge of the market. Highland cattle were growing in demand, especially in the Borders, as the market rose steadily. John Spottiswoode showed his awareness of this by building a Shade (or shed) to shelter them in winter. Until the middle years of the century, cattle often had to fend for themselves outside. Many died, causing great hardship, especially in the north where starvation caused much distress in winter. Andrew Cribbis continued to work at the quarry, the Deanbrae Quarry the Laird points out, which is mainly whinstone. But he also tried to build up his little farm by buying two young sows. The boar died and Andrew Cribbis bought part of it, either to eat or salt down. He was granted a new farm for a rent of £4 a year. This was perhaps the reason why there were no more entries against his name. Better prices and a greater demand for farm produce might have persuaded him to farm fulltime.

In 1770 John Spottiswoode described an experiment which he carried out to try and improve the fertility of his ground. It was the first time he had written at such length: 'Mr. Riddle at Dod's House in Lauderdale had got some people in Alnwick in Northumberland to cast or pair some of his muirs. I went in the end of May to see their work in company with

John Gray in Blainslie & as I thought it more advantageous than plowing, I would try it. so I desired one of them to come and see my grounds. Thos Hewat came and I agreed with him at 16/– ster. p. acre. They came at the end of June and although they lived in England I soon discovered they were all Scots or of Scots extract. Two of them were from this County, particularly Archd Cromie from Greenlaw & Thos. Hewat. His Father was presently serving at Stainrigg. They paired inde [sic] £16. But as they did not burn I hired Thos Gray for that at 5/– [an acre?]. This I thought very expensive.

'1771. I sent to Ro. Troler at Morpeth for 6 pairing spades which cost me with carriage £1. 3. 2d. and engaged my own men with some oyrs [others] to pair and burn at 15/– p. acre. They pared and burnt 13.09558 [acres] and made very good wages £9 16s. 4d. Gave Hewat when he came to look at the ground 2/6 Paid for the spades with carriage £1. 3. 2d. 3/6 each spade. Both these ways are expensive but much labour and time is saved as one can have a crop 2 years sooner of muir grounds than by common plowing. I sowed the above 20 acres in March '71 but whether it was the dry summer or the land not being well broke with once plowing I had no crop, not my seed in return!' A few years later he might well have had a crop after spending so much money on lime.

In 1760 Jo. Neil 'entered my service to drive the plow at 18/4d for the half year. In '61 he came in as a boy for the house at £2 sterling yearly wages. At Whitsun '63 his wages were advanced to £2. 12/–. At Whitsun '65 he got the charge of the stable and drove the Chaise and his wages were advanced to £5 ster. At Whitsun '66 he received the above wages 1 house Cow's grass summer and winter beside 6 sheeps grass which I had given him for some years past and he was married in June '66 to Peggie Dick who had formerely been a servant in the house. His wages due preceeding Whitsun 1762 paid his father and himself'. (His father was John Neil, the miller.) As the Laird said, Jo. Neil was married to Peggie Dick, and it must have been a matter of some envy among the young folk to see her marry the Spottiswoode chaise driver. He would be popular, too, with the older generations as he borrowed £1 13s. 4d. from the Laird 'for 20 pints of Wiskie to his marriage'. Hardly a Penny

Wedding! For the next six years Jo. Neil worked away with no adverse comment from the Laird. He grew some crop, ran a few sheep and, of course, drove the chaise to Edinburgh when the Laird had business there. On these visits he borrowed money from his Master, no doubt to buy a few trinkets and necessities. In 1774 his sister was married but Jo. Neil was a responsible man now and only drew 5s. against his wages for that celebration. When he went to Edinburgh two months later, he borrowed one guinea! In 1777 he bought from the Laird '1 stirk brought up from a calf until she gave milk' for £1. This was his final transaction with the Laird. No reason was given for his leaving, but he left a fine signature.

James Allan came to work at Spottiswoode in 1765 and the Laird writes: 'He was Son to Jo Allan and Tibbie Jaffery who nursed four of my children, viz, Thomson, Nelly, Annie and Jennie who dyed young. He came to my service betwixt terms in January 1765 as a plowman and had herded to me one summer formerely his wages to Whitsun 1765 was £1. 10/– In April '65 I agreed with him to serve me for another year, viz, to Whitsun '66 at £5 without any shoes. In March 1766 I agreed with him for another year at the above wages, six sheeps Grass in place of shoes'.

'Nota: The 7th Jully he marryed Willie Kirkwood's daughter Peggie and I agreed with him to serve me as formerely for another year at £4 ster, a cow's grass, free house, the above sheeps grass and 6 bolls meal for his meat so he goes out of ye house this day and has got 1 boll meal the time from Whitsun to be discounted'. The Laird was clearly keen to retain James Allan's service. So it must have been with some sorrow that the Laird wrote: 'He left my service 27th, May 1772'. James Allan had been given (or allowed) timber to form a chimney in his house so that it would not smoke. He had to have it valued since he was leaving and his account had to be cleared. So Wm. Haig examined it and declared it worth 7s. 6d. This was duly deducted from what James Allan was owed, i.e. £15 16s. His signature at the bottom of his account is bold and well formed.

14

Spottiswoode in Transition

IT IS NOW POSSIBLE to see from the Diary that up to about 1750–1755 John Spottiswoode was still able to dictate the level of remuneration which his employees received. Scotland was a poor nation and although there were encouraging stirrings, mainly in industry, there was no great increase in the numbers of men needed on the land. Farming was still conducted along the sterile lines which landowners and the farm touns had followed for centuries. Indeed, some of the methods used were based on superstition. The low yield from cereals, mainly oats, and still the staple food of the people, was summed up by the ancient saying 'Ane grain to saw, ane tae gnaw and ane tae gie the Laird witha'.'

Cattle were reared in a most primitive fashion and many were so puny and weak they were lucky to realise £1 per head at the Crieff and Falkirk Trysts. Despite the fact that poorly bred beasts brought in very little money, nothing was ever done to improve their methods of rearing.

Sheep in the north were also poor stunted little beasts and in the south little better. In this depressed state of affairs, therefore, the wage for a farm servant was no more than 6d. a day. So farming methods remained primitive and men who worked on the land appeared sullen and dejected, shorn of all ambition with only a subsistence standard of living as their lot. If they found work they tended to stay where they found it because if they left, there was nothing but starvation ahead of them. The memories of bands of beggars roaming the countryside searching for food and unable to find even the most menial work would be told and re-told by their parents, over and over again. But all this did was increase the general depression and make the battle against poverty harder to bear.

But 10 years after the '45 Uprising, conditions slowly began to improve. A man no longer had to stay with one employer throughout his working life. He began to find other work which paid better and he could buy a greater variety of food. But, although he could not improve his standard of living all at once, he seemed to know that one day he would. For this reason he was not content to hold on to the same employment for 25 or 30 years as his forefathers did, and this is reflected in the Diary/Journal very clearly indeed. It also reflects the Laird's unease at the changing situation and his need to write down in far greater detail what he thought of his men. But he is also fair-minded and this is fully borne out in his remarks about the nursing of his children. With change pouring over the farms like a rising torrent, the Laird battles on against the flood and does his utmost to remain in control. However, at times, he seems exasperated beyond measure.

Archibald Vallange was an older man and arrived at Spottiswoode in 1764. He brought his son with him, both of them being paid 6d. a day. As expected, their duties varied from working at the turnpike road to cutting hay and 'cleaning the Muir of stones'. His wife and daughter were employed at the usual task for women – shearing the harvest of 1764 and '65 while he cast divots and looked after the Long Walk, the Piper Walk and the Orchard. But after giving details of those, the Laird seems to engage in a little cheating. Vallange is told to work at 'the sheep folds', meaning build them up and repair the gaps for which he receives a rate of 1d. a rood. Then the Laird adds this: 'Nota. The Common price is 10d. p. rood'. But he then adds what appears to be compensation to Vallange whose job it now was to repair the 'Nolt folds'. These were cattle pens, similar to sheep pens, but larger and stronger. Their existence at Spottiswoode indicates there were a number of cattle on the estate, certainly enough to justify folds or pens, where they could be handled. The Laird writes: 'He gets double bounteth for these'. This means double bounties or a bonus. Bounties varied from place to place and could be paid either in money or produce or clothing. Vallange buys several lots of hay from the Laird – from which it would seem he ran some cattle of his own including cows. This is borne out by the sale to the Laird of 11lbs of butter for smearing. But strangely, he does not ask for more than 6d. per lb – the price James Rutherfoord charged several years earlier.

Vallange was not employed at Spottiswoode for long, which was obviously through his own fault. 'I turned him off my work [in October, 1768] for breaking down the fences and making roads through them.' This was all too common on estates at this time. Tenants rarely looked after their grazing, with the result it became poorer and poorer. Consequently, hungry cattle and sheep continually broke through the dykes whenever they could. Tenants did as little as possible to prevent them from doing so, as the Laird's grazing was better than theirs and there was always far more of it. Allowing cattle and sheep through, especially at night, was too tempting to be resisted. The Laird was a typical canny Scot and hated having to pay again and again for work done, as was necessary each time his dykes were 'thrown down'.

Vallange is a strange name. It does not appear in any local 1992 Directory, although Vallance does. Vallance also appears in the lime record for the Spottiswoode Estate.

Adam Hope 'Entered to my service in quality of Barn Man in 1767 at £2 for the half year and 3/– for shoes and his diet within the House. His Father is Herd in Harlaw'. Adam must have pleased the Laird because he was hired again in 1768 and '69, although he demanded two or three sheep's grass as stocking. He was to drive a lime cart all summer and look after four horses. The next year he was to drive a stone cart and look after his horse and do any work. He left in 1780 and went to Torwoodlie.

James Melrose came in 1767 as a gardener, 'His wage to be £5 per year, with 6 bolls of meal, a free house and Cow's grass, summer and winter with fodder and his peats led as the other servants that are without the House'. The Laird was not impressed by Melrose but the gentler side of his nature came to the fore when 'He got 1 firlot of malt but as he is poor and had no cow, till the Whitsun and his sister weeded in the yard some days in summer '67, I don't charge it'. However, at the end of that year, 1768, the Laird gave him the cash to buy a cow at Jo. Lillie's roup and this cost him £5 11s. 1d., which was more than his year's wage. He was also given one guinea 'When his wife was in labour'. This would be to pay for all the women who assisted at the birth.

When a child was born, especially in country districts, the people were convinced it lay in immediate danger of being spirited away by fairies and a changeling left in its place. Women therefore kept watch all night, walking round the bed with a Bible in their hands and wishing all evil spirits to begone to the Red Sea! Only after the christening were the new-born child and its anxious mother freed from this danger. All this cost the father money, added to which was the cost of entertaining his family and friends. By the time James Melrose's child was safely christened, there would be little or nothing left of the guinea he borrowed.

Melrose went to Edinburgh a year later and borrowed 5s. from the Laird. The purpose of this visit 'was to hire', i.e. put himself on the feeing market to which lairds and farmers came to hire labour, usually for the next six months but sometimes for a year. He must have found work because the Laird dismissed him in November, 1769, adding this: 'Nota. He left my service this day he was an indifferent Workman & never kept anything clean which made me dismiss him. He had some ground this year but as his acre last year was dear I took nothing for it'. James Melrose signed the Laird's Ledger in a beautiful flowing style.

Alexander Sanderson came in 1769, describing himself as a gardener. John Spottiswoode was in a difficulty here. With every improvement he made to his grounds, more work was needed to keep them tidy. But gardeners were still a scarce breed and there was much competition for them. The famous Improver, John Cockburn of Ormiston, had to go to Tottenham in London to find his gardener, Charles Bell. However, any man seemed better than James Melrose, so in an obvious attempt to encourage him, he gave Sanderson £6 a year right away – £1 more than Melrose, his food and his washing within the house. 'He was marryed but not discovered till Jully '70. So at Martinmas '70 he brought home his wife and has a cow's grass and foddered all the winter 6 bolls meal free house and firing led home.' Then comes a strange entry: 'To cash paid to Mr. Cockburn Writer to ye Signet . . . £3. 3/–'. In March a further £3 was drawn 'for Lauder Fair'. After four years, there was not a single entry, indicating that Sanderson had sold goods against his purchases of £23 2/–. However, he was accused of an 'oversum' (i.e. over-grazing on the Laird's muir) and debited £1. In May of 1775, he drew £1 'when his wife lay in', and he bought 100 herring for 2s. This alone showed how inflation was beginning to show itself. In October of 1777, he had to draw £1 when 'His wife was delivered of a son'. And a further 10s. the following May 'At the death of his son'. As with the other men who had recently served the Laird, Alex Sanderson left his employ at the November term of 1778.

In his place, Joseph Maben came on a year's contract; his wages 'Including meal is to be Ten Guineas a cow's grass in summer and winter fodder a free house and his elding led home to him'. Elding was fuel and could be any article which would burn, i.e. peat, the mature branches of whin bushes, fallen dead branches and dried grasses. Up to the late '70s elding had not figured in the men's wages, a further indication of the rising cost of skilled labour. The Laird then tells us: 'Maben's father is a feuer and weaver at Newstead, near Melrose and he was himself long in England and sometime in Blenheim and many other capital Gardens. He was last with Sir James Douglas, Springwood Park near Kelso'. Was this a tale to impress the Laird? It might well have been. The Laird had to reimburse him 'For 6 Apply Trees' which Maben had bought at Kelso during a visit in September of '79. But the Laird kept him waiting three months before he paid for them! Then comes another Nota: 'I agreed with him for another year and augmented his wages 2 guineas, so after Martinmas his wages for next year are £12. 12/–'. It is possible to detect John Spottiswoode's growing concern at Joseph Maben. His patience broke in July of 1780. 'He in his wonted imprudent manner most impudently broke down the fence at ye watering place in the park below ye lawn which not a moneth before had cost me two men and a cart for about a week puting up and as no reproofs will mend him for this offence, I charge 5/–'!

A month later, matters came to a head. 'I was obliged to turn him off for impertinence and giving saucey language when kitchen staff was asked from him etc etc. He is the first servant I ever turned off mid term in my life. He flitted to Dalkeith, the common shore of all my discarded servants'!

That was followed by a more peaceful entry: 'W. Waddle brought from Anderson [the] Nurseryman, Gilbert Ross at 6d. a day bed and board but not washing. He is a Shire of Air man been eight years in England and is to stay some weeks if we do not agree for a longer time'. There was no agreement and Gilbert Ross left, his brother collecting the money due and signing for it in a fine neat hand.

Prior to the upset with James Maben, there had been a furious encounter with James Cribbis. The Laird writes: 'After Whitsun, I was obliged to make short work with Jas Cribbis. He never was a faithfull Servant but he at this time was guilty of fraud in making my meal and in causing upset to Craw the Miller's bairns and give McFarlan ill language in order to cover his fraud which made me Turn him off. I wanted one in his place the moneths of June, Jully and part of August. Ro. Binnie recommended John Sclater who had served Bemmerside several years and was working with Mr. Hay of Hopes at Drygrange (near Earlston). He brought him and I agreed to give him £5 wages, a free house, 1 cow summer and winter till Whitsun 1772, with 6 bolls of meal. On Tuesday, 20 August Jo Sclater came for carts to bring his furniture. On 22nd, he and his Family came and next day he entered to work in racking hay. On 7th April 1772 I agreed with Jo Sclater for another year after Whitsun. He is to have £5 wages, 6 shillings for two pairs of shoes and I am to give him the ground James Cribbis had last year and sow it with oats of my own, but if he sows bear he provides the seed himself & his meal, cow's grass as formerely. I also agreed with him for his son Willie to drive the plough for one year after Whitsun, his wages 25 shillings sterling, 6 shillings for shoes and 6 bolls meal but nothing for kitchen'. In this case 'driving' meant goading the beasts into pulling the big, heavy Scots plough, this being regarded all over as a boy's job. Small's plough had not yet been introduced at Spottiswoode.

At this time, most Improvers bought Highland cattle with which to stock their farms. They would cost between £3 and £12 depending on quality. But they were hardy brutes and could stand a great deal of rough weather and this was their main attraction. John Sclater took a half share in a Highland cow which cost him £1. 7. 6d. He also took a half share in a sow and this cost 2s. 6d. A bushel of salt cost him 2d. more. The following year, he took another half share with Jo. Neil in a young swine, costing 5s. this time. He was a regular visitor to the local Fairs, going to Edinburgh in September where he spent 2s. 5d., and then to Lauder Fair in October where he spent 5s., then Kelso Fair the following August when he drew 6s. 6d. and Lauder again the next October where he spent 4s. 1d. He then bought 330 herrings from the Laird for 6s. 6d. and another young pig for 5s. But the Laird could see from his account that the gap between what Sclater earned and what he spent was growing wider, even though many of the items he bought were at Fairs and were largely livestock. To help out, perhaps, he was allowed to bring his other son Wattie to work for £2 10s. for the year, 10s. more than Will. Then the Laird made this entry: 'To deduction from Will for absence, being at school'. During 1776, the Sclater family worked hard and spent little so that by the end of 1777 they owed the Laird £38 and he owed them £45. However, there was another son, Robert, who was getting married in Edinburgh and caused his father to draw £2 2s.

Just when John Sclater and his sons appeared to be better established at Spottiswoode, having several animals, the Laird made this entry: 'To cash this day of £1. 10. 5d, when he left my service'. But the books did not balance. The Laird still owed John Sclater £13 and sent it in two instalments via Wm. Waddle. But it took over six months to pay what he owed. No reason was given why John Sclater left.

Hugh Foreman came to take land at Hardacres and, as was customary, hired himself to the Laird when time allowed. He was paid the usual 6d. per day. He also had to put his house in order and bought 5,500 divots at 1s. per thousand. He also bought 700 'fail' which were turves used to form the roof. The Laird must have found Hugh a congenial man as the Journal makes no criticism of him. After four years, he must have had at least one cow as he sold John Spottiswoode 19lbs of butter 'but only 18 libb payable'. One wonders what was wrong with the pound deducted. If the butter was for eating, it may have had too many hairs or was too rancid. But if it was for smearing sheep, the hairs would not matter. In many places, hair in butter was said to improve the quality! Foreman was obviously concerned by the condition of his door lock as the Laird credited him 6d. 'for mending it'. He bought two 'shiks' from the Laird, these being small stacks either of hay or straw. They only cost him 1s. 3d. and were possibly for his house floor. Then came a little barter – a dead hog in exchange for a 'Bee skape'. The lack of a good gardener made John Spottiswoode engage all manner of labour to keep his grounds as he wanted them. Hugh Foreman looked after '16 borders in the Orchard'. He also helped the planting of 7,820 firs and 1350 beeches as well as pitting 330 firs. After that he prepared 382 pits for acorns (the Laird spells them 'Alcorns') and pays 9d. per long hundred. There was also 'half a hundred Spruce Firs pitted in ye Pikie park'. Hugh Foreman left in May, 1770, but again no reason is given.

William Brown was entered at Spottiswoode in May 1764 and was attached to a gang of five others. They had a big task on hand, described by the Laird. 'By himself, George Peacock and other 4 men in casting the march ditch betwixt Thorndyke and me begun this day (being Thursday) at ye burn above ye Pyetshaw near oppsite ye Dods and running east till it enter ye Jordanlaw Moss at ye foot of ye eastmost muir park being, per agreemt to be 8 foot wide at 1/– per rood which was ended by them Wednesday 26 September and measured 29 September 1764 by Jas. Hewat, Tenant in Flas [farm]'. It amounted to 614 roods and cost John Spottiswoode £15 7s. But he added cautiously: 'Nota: The chain by which it was measured consists of 60 links and every link 1 foot'. It later became 22 yards, i.e. 66 feet, and is still the measurement of a cricket pitch and called 'A Chain'. At seven yards to the rood, this ditch was 4298 yards long and thus able to carry away a great deal of water. In addition to that, the Laird had a stretch of road 'formed, westside of Pyetshaw burn till it meets with the Turnpike road and [is] stoned and graveled. The total cost was about £57 ster.' Then another Nota: 'beside the above, there was about 60 rood stoned and graveled by myself with my own carts some hired and some gratis'. It had taken over a year to complete all this. But the Laird still had something more to say, because

Hewat's measure (on which the men were paid) was found to be less than that of Cribbis. Another reason for not having trusted him!

At the end of 1766, William Brown was allowed to enter his father to work on the estate. He mainly drove a cart with stones for the dykers. Nevertheless, the Laird warns: 'He did not get the crop at his entering and therefore has it at his removeall'. This was the old way. When a man took ground as a tenant he was given barley or oat seed, a cow and grazing and possibly some hay and straw. This was a kind way of giving him a helping hand. But at his 'removeall' he was not allowed to take his final crop. It belonged to the Laird. This is what William Brown had agreed with John Spottiswoode. Throughout that year Brown and his father worked mainly on roads. But in January of 1770 William was sent to Berwick, 'Bringing and carrying back Betty Gourly himself and horse', for which he was paid 5s. Was she taking a place in the house?

At the end of 1770, William Brown owed the Laird £89 1s. 9d. and John Spottiswoode owed him £68 2s. 4d. He would have taken note of this gap and decided how to deal with it, namely, set William Brown to drainage work, the making of 'cundies or Sivers', leading stones, working at the freestone quarry and building or repairing dykes. But he also planted trees. He put in 1,500 firs at 1s. per long hundred and then 'led stones for the great Circle on the top of Brotherfield muir'. At the end of the year, he had reduced his debt to John Spottiswoode to £12. But he and the Laird were square by the end of 1783, which is quite surprising as each of them had traded with the other, either in goods or in services to the tune of £275 – by far the largest amount in the whole of the Diary/Journal. It is a pity, however, that the Laird does not give his opinion of Brown.

William Dickson 'Entered into my service 18 Jully 1763 at £3 ster wages [per year] 6 bolls meal and 4d. per week for kitchen which is 17/4d p. year & to pay for his house and 1/6 per head for what sheep he should have of his own on ye ground'. He worked without comment to 16 March, 1771 and apparently gave no trouble. But there is another indication of an inflationary tendency in the price Dickson paid for herring, viz. 2s. for 100. Not many years before, the price was 1s. 4d. for 200. On the other hand, Dickson received 4d. per week for his kitchen as well as paying 5s. for his shoes when these had been available at half that money. By the end of 1782 he owed the Laird £69 17s. 11d. and the Laird owed him £68 19s. 4d. He had built himself up with a flock of 19 sheep and at least one cow and possibly a calf or two. John Spottiswoode does not say why he left.

John Hendrie began work at the November term 1766 and was paid on a daily basis. On the other hand, he asked for and received one guinea when the Laird went to Galloway. At this point he was certainly being paid daily wages at the usual rate of 6d. a day. But he seems to have been able to do any kind of work from digging ditches and baxes and cleaning riggs to helping to set up the Whale Bones. There is a full description in the Laird's hand of how this job was done in November 1767. But only after this preliminary notice of them are Hendry's terms of employment given, though not until he had been ordered to dig pits for the planting of ash trees in the East Park at 2d. a score 'Which I begin to think was too much and that 1d. was enough. But as he was a Miller to trade he got £5 sterling & a pair of double shoes to work Allanbank mill for half a year so he went off my work for the sake of this great wage'. But then comes a little Nota in the margin: 'He returned in harvest to work'. Return he did and was given 10,800 firs to plant with Hugh Foreman. After that, there were 2,700 beeches to put in and a further 60 spruce firs to pit. Then just to show his eye was everywhere, he charged John Hendrie 6d. for losing a hoe. From that work, he was switched to 'Coping and failing part of the Great Circle in the Brotherfield Muir'.

John Spottiswoode often appears to be driven along by his determination to bring perfection to his gardens and grounds. An example of this comes under the name of Robert Binnie, 'A Wright in Newstead, near Melrose'. He was engaged 'in order to make a Chinese Rail for the sweep at the West Avenue'. But first, Robert Binnie had to make a new manger for the bull and put up new trevises. Neither of these seems to have been paid for. Trevises were the partitions between tethered animals. Binnie brought with him his 'prentice and his journeyman and, being a wright, he would need the help of both. The Laird obviously agreed.

Six months went by before Robert Binnie began work on the Chinese

Rail and other items such as the smiddy roofs and putting glass in the windows of the millhouses. At this time, timber was still very scarce because the Laird sent Binnie to buy wood and pay 'Postage of 2 letters'. Somehow Binnie managed to get hold of a single plank of elm wood and sold this for 8s. to John Spottiswoode who decided to use it for his barley mill.

Meantime, he was hiring John Fair, 'prentice in his first year, at 7d. a day. A second 'prentice, George Vere, was hired for 8d. In November of that year, 1772, the Laird sold Binnie a Highland cow at Melrose Fair for £3. Binnie then had to repair the waggonhouse roof and after that cut 21 stabbs for the paling at Blyth March. In view of these special tasks, there was a full programme facing Robert Binnie, his 'prentices and journeymen. One item was 'Cutting trees and breaking 'em out for cart graith at Newstead in January or February, 1777'. This was a roundabout way of saying everything was ready, the wood cut, measured and prepared and the wheels made and everything furnished. Then a different job: 'By sawing of plaister lath, 50 dales [these were deals or soft wood boards] and 16 trees for paleing [wooden rails] at ye planting at Hexpath Toll Bar'. This is interesting because it appears to be one of the first times the Laird cut timber from his new plantations.

But work was going on elsewhere on the estate and we observe that Robert Binnie had to set up the posts in the new stables. These buildings are still standing and are a very handsome range. Robert Binnie remained at Spottiswoode for over 10 years and it is clear from the variety of tasks he was given that his workmanship was good. Then comes a Nota: 'The Kiln at Bruntaburn Mill was burnt on Friday 26th. November occasioned by a high wind when drying corn to Wm. Shiel in Wood-hall. His journeyman, James Paton wrought 9 days repairing her at 9d. with victuals', i.e. 9d. per day with food. Robert Binnie then went to Leith for 'Timber and Nails'. The timber situation was still critical in southern Scotland, and those who had planted trees were still waiting for them to grow tall enough to cut. The best place from which to import was either Leith or one of the other east-coast ports. They had an established trade in timber with Scandinavia, and landowners like John Spottiswoode could

order what they needed from any Leith timber merchant. The Diary
records that this timber was for Walter Iddington's houses. This was a
respected tenant of the Laird, paying him £50 a year in rent for the large
farm at Westruther (Mains).

So far in the Diary there has been very little mention of house couples,
but, in fact, almost all the houses on the estate would be roughly built
with stones collected off the fields and made up into walls about five feet
high. Timbers called couples were then set into these walls. These were
composed of two pieces of wood, usually some 8 to 10 feet in length and
secured to each other at the top, making a figure 'A'. The roof of sods
or heather was then cut and laid between the couples and held down with
grass ropes, weighted with stones. When a man left his place of work to
take up a position elsewhere, he took his couples with him, leaving his
successor nothing but four crumbling walls and possibly a door and a
single opening as a window. The fact that Walter Iddington was building
new houses must not be taken to mean he was building them in stone
with slated roofing. However, it is a possibility, judging from what the
Laird wrote in the Diary: 'By laying the floor of the large house betwixt
the 2 Shades. [It is a] 45 Couple room at 15d per Couple, workmanship,
nails and timber being furnished'.

The final lines concerning Robert Binnie are worth noting: 'To Lime
furnished for your use to Thornydyke house in Jully last [this was now
November] and to a piece of dale [white wood] furnished him. To a fat
wedder . . . 11/–'. John Spottiswoode does not say where he went, but
as Robert Binnie had his own business which would likely be flourishing
at this time, he would take his final payment of £25 4s. 6d. and look
elsewhere for work.

John Nicol was another farm servant who took up work at Spottiswoode
in 1770. The Laird records that he came from Birkhillside on 2nd January
at 8d. a day and the usual other benefits in kind. He then adds this nice
touch: 'As the Gardiner's house was empty, I brought his wife and part
of his furniture to it, the end of the month'. He then adds an important
Nota: ' From the time I began work which was about the 1743 till now,
I only gave 6d. per day but for some time past I have been very ill served

and was obliged last year to make a Tottal change of my workmen except James Rutherford who has grown superannuate in my service having wrought with me at 6d. a day since Whitsun 1747 and as ye wages for some years past has been very high I am now obliged to augment mine to these I have taken on this year to 8d.'. But what the Laird does not say is that he regarded a bargain as unbreakable, so that if a man signed on at 6d. a day, he stayed at that wage until he either died or left. Meantime, he has more to add concerning John Nicol. 'Nota: As this was his first year he got his acre and so at his removeall he either does not get it or if he gets it he has to pay for it after he goes away.' It was the long established way, in other words the steelbow system. Nicol was immediately involved in planting 33,500 firs during March and April and after this backbreaking job he would have been disappointed at receiving only 12s. 6d. as his share. But Nicol must have been a worker because the Laird noted that he had sown his acre's crop and reaped it. He also bought hay at the roup for 15s. Then comes an intriguing little remark: 'To cash given to him by Miss Nellie'. Was this the Laird's daughter Helen? It is more than likely because it would appear that two people were now writing up the Diary.

In 1772, John Nicol bought a fair quantity of hay at the Spottiswoode roup because it cost him £1 2s. This can only mean it was probably better hay than he could make himself and that he had at least one cow and calf to keep. His work for the next wee while was paring and burning two acres of the muir. Here, it would seem, the Laird drove too hard a bargain. Having found the experiment at Dod House in May 1770 too expensive, he cut the wage right down to his own men, who, knowing no better, accepted it. But just to make certain, he noted that he was paying them 10s. per acre for paring and 5s. per acre for burning. Compared to the wage the men received who pared and burnt the 20 acres at Dod, John Spottiswoode's terms to his own men were miserly indeed. Finally he credits John Nicol for 'His maid burning in ye muir' and pays her 7d.

James Nisbet also came from Birkhillside in 1770. By this time, the Laird doesn't trouble to state the terms on which he would work. They appear later as if they were an afterthought. However, his first work was to cut 38,000 divots at 1s. a thousand. The Laird then puts a Nota in the margin: 'He has an acre when he flits as he got none at his entry'. This shows how firmly held these ancient agreements were. Nisbet came from the same place as Nicol, Birkhillside, so they knew each other. This is why the Laird put them together and set them to paring and burning the muir. Later, Nisbet pared and burnt himself and was paid for 3.5 acres. Then in December 1773 'He dyed of a fever', and the Laird adds: 'He was a very good workman and well natured'. But it was July 1777 before his widow received what her husband was owed. It included 1s. 4d. 'For 1 dyker spade' which she sold the Laird.

The next man to look for work at Spottiswoode was a most unusual person. In the Laird's own words: 'He was a soldier and was 9 years in North America and has the Chelsea Pension. He came from Chappel. He dyed Sunday 1st September, 1771 of a fever very much regrated He was an understanding Workman & had been a soldier Was at the taking of Havanna and 9 years in Canada and was a Chelsea Pensioner'. It is a measure of the Laird's shock that he repeats himself here. Although he does not say so, Robert Wadderston was probably at the taking of Quebec, which victory opened the way for the capture of Canada. In any event, John Spottiswoode admired him and this is borne out by his trying to give the widow some work as well as paying her what was due to her husband before he died. There were 130 days at the regulation 8d. a day and then a different kind of entry: 'By his weeding the Nursery. As it was not finished at his death 10/– is deducted'. The Laird then bought from his widow: '1 How [hoe] and Mattock for 3/– and 1 Ach for 2/4d'. Might this have been the log of an ash tree?

Three farm servants came and went after brief service with the Laird. First there was James Jaffray who entered as 'Plowman' and was dismissed 27th May, 1777. But the Laird gave him all he was owed, viz. £14 5s. after five years. Jaffray signed the book in a handsome hand.

David Spence came two weeks later as a household servant at £4 sterling (per year) and his clothes. The Laird recorded his view of matters: 'This day [15th May, 1779] paid him £2 sterling as the Ballce [balance] of his two years wages'. David Spence's signature was much less bold. The

Laird adds this comment: 'He left my service and went to Sir John Dalrymple, Baron in Exchequer. Broke his service and went to Lord Traquair at Martinmas, 1779'.

Robert Redpath entered as labouring servant at Whitsun 1779. He came from John Carter. His wages were £5 8s. including shoes. He left in 1781 and John Spottiswoode says this: 'He did his work peaceably and was a good servant'. His signature was clear but untidy.

Adam Dick entered as 'Plow Boy' at Martinmas 1776 but was taken in to serve the house 'and continued till this Term [May 1784]. His wages were small at first but from time to time augmented at Whitsun last, '83. He drove the Chaise and had charge of ye horses in place of Wm Waddle. His wages for this last year were £5. 15/–. He left my service out of greed and pride that Wm Waddle was more noticed than him. He went to one Mrs Gordon, a widow lady at Edinburgh, his Mother, a widow, lives in Fans'. He left a clear signature and departed Spottiswoode in May, 1784.

One of the men who had taken part in the experiment of paring and burning, which had taken place at Dods, was ditcher and day labourer, Thomas Gray, from Earlestown. According to the Laird, 'His father had been the Edinburgh Currier and he himself continued the trade but finding it not answer went to England and wrought at Muir burning after it was pared and other labouring work and when I got the parers from Mr. Riddle he came and offered himself to burn it'. So, 20 acres of pared muir near the Great Circle were burnt by Gray for which he earned £5. Being a ditcher, Gray was then sent to trench '7 walks in The Great Circle on the top of the muir, being 133 roods [i.e. 930 yards] and the small center circle from which these walks go off'. This is important in view of the excavation work on the Great Circle ordered by Lady Alicia Anne Scott Spottiswoode. She was convinced this circle was of Pictish origin but nothing was ever found to support this contention. The reason is now obvious.

There were other jobs Gray had to do, viz. 'weeding the Potatoe crop in July of '71'; and, as he must have done it well, he was ordered to do it again the following year. It took him four days which indicates several acres, especially as a day in summer began at first light and went on until 8 or 9 o'clock at night. Having finished his weeding, Gray was told to 'Dig at the Well for a pump well'. This appears to be still there, beautifully built in stone, some 10 feet deep and with steps down to water level. The pumping would possibly be done by two men with poles. That work finished, Gray went to the Whinstone Quarry 'To help the Masons', and then to help mow 15 acres of hay with Alec Forsyth. After that came the 'Cleaning of ye Birch and thorn hedges on both sides of the stripe on ye south side of ye road from Paddowhall gate to Pyetshaw march dyke'. It is the first time the Laird has used the word 'Gate' instead of 'Yett'. Then comes another interesting entry: 'By trenching ye Walk in the westmost Circle at ye Obelisk'.

William Hardie from Blainslee (now spelt Blainslie) entered in 1776 and the Laird has this to say of him: 'He served the Masons at the new Barn in the 1770 and took Ro. Waterston's house at Hardacres. As he had taken John Shiells possession at the Mason's Lodge whose Wife made him give up his bargain, I refused to bring his plenishings at such a distance as I had a horse lamed in bringing John Shiels from Bowling. He brought it on his own charge. I did not think of employing him as he seemed good for nothing but to serve Masons But Andrew Graham's houses being to repair immediately at his coming which was Whitsun I was necessitate to take him in and have now set him Ro. Watherstons possession'. There are two points here. Firstly, the Laird had taken a dislike to Hardie apparently on sight and the other was that Hardie was able to take the deceased Watherston's house, which meant that the widow had left. What happened to her is conjecture but without a husband she would have great difficulty in finding work, unless she could take a post as a servant in one of the mansionhouses in the district. But the rule of the time was absolute – no wage earner, no house.

Looking over the tasks Hardie was ordered to perform, it is clear he had many unpleasant jobs to do. He had to prise out stones in the Bog of Pyetshaw and do general outside work through the winter of 1772. When one remembers that most of this would be done in bare feet, it is a wonder anyone could stand it. But Hardie did and drew a grudging comment from the Laird: 'Nota: There was 63 stone raggs cut for 4/–, per agreement. He cut 'em in about 5 days'. It is not clear what the Laird means by 'raggs' unless they are stones prepared for winnowing.

That done, Hardie had to take his share of 'digging stones in five different places of the muir at Rockieknold park during the winter of '72'. Then comes an unusual phrase: 'To the pasture of 2 Nolt during the winter'. Nolt can refer to either horses or cattle but the important thing is that Hardie had two to fodder over the winter because the Laird charged him 5s. each. They were obviously left outside to fend for themselves, but provided there was some shelter and enough rough herbage, they would survive. Hardie was already building up his capital.

Meantime he was set to help the masons again. He had to level 299 square yards of the close and serve the man who laid the paving outside the house. He then had a calf to sell and the Laird took it for 18s. It is a strange amount and suggests some haggling. But in 1774 it was back to the rough jobs. In January Hardie was ordered to clean and redd-up the whinstone quarry at Pyetshaws. This would be dusty at most times, and the sharp stone pieces on the floor of the quarry would make walking painful.

Hardie had a son and as soon as he was old enough to work the Laird took him on, sending him to help the gardener. He then had him help the shearing of the harvest of 1776 at 5d. a day. After that he was sent to herd the Highland cows at 6d. a day. One wonders whether he was afraid of them with their big menacing horns. Meantime, Hardie was given another very dirty job – that of smearing sheep. But at the end of that he was offered a Highland cow with calf by the Laird and took them for £4 7s. Again, this is an unusual price and indicates haggling. The following Spring, 1777, Hardie's son was given the task of herding the ewes at 9d. per week. Given such a low wage, this is possibly a younger son. If so, the older boy would possibly be at school. Now comes the final entry for Hardie. 'By Ballce due by William Hardie and paid this 27th. February 1778 – £1. 15. 7d. He left me at Whitsun 1777 and took a farm from Lord Lauderdale in company with Wm. Bower'.

Alexander Forsyth (the Laird spells it Forthsyth) came to Spottiswoode in 1772 and John Spottiswoode describes him. '[He] was of this Parish some years ago. He was hired by The Trustees for Manufactories and to go to the Shire of Ross. They engaged him for 5 years at £15 ster. yearly for meal and wage. Their design in this was to teach the Highlanders the art of Husbandry but they would not foresake their old customs and were little the better at the end of the five years The Trustees withdrew the sallary and he came home. He says he would have had 40 miles to go for a boll of meal for which he paid a guinea. After he came home, Lord Blantyre engaged him for his plowman in the west country at Erskine. In the Spring 1772 his wife took the porter lodge and after he cam home he wrought sometimes to me and as he seemed a good workman he continued part of that year. He was given the skilled work of building a sheep fold in the muir – without meal or bounteth. He dug out 13,000 divots for the Mill houses and received 1/– a day for thatching them. Next he did the same for Thimblehall House'.

In the winter of 1774 the Laird 'Agreed with him to hold one of the plows and to fodder and take care of the cows'. But he must have decided to leave because John Spottiswoode noted: 'I gave him 2 Kelso caps of bear which he alleged was owing for his flitting crop. I did not think by the verbal bargain I made with him it was due as he had no sowing the first year by his bargain and mine but as he was a poor man and witless fellow I gave it him rather than hear him complaining, so it was rather out of charity'!

The following are entries for 'Labouring Servants':

1. William Waddle, Son to John Waddle, Weaver in Bassendean. Rented a large farm at £112 p.a. Name not known. Entered Home as Gad Boy May '72. Wages £2 and 6 shillings for shoes the whole year.

2. James Jaffray, nephew to the nurse entered as Plowman 30 May '72. Wages £4. 15/– and 6 shillings for shoes the whole year.

3. Robert Brown, son to the late Taylor Tom entered as Carter or Plowman 1st June '72. Wages £4 and 6 shillings for shoes the whole year. Optional to part at Martinmas. He was so good for nothing I set him off at Martinmas.

4. Adam Kay, son to John Kay, late Tenant in Bassendean, part of

Westruther entered home 25th. November, 1772. Wages for year £2. 10/− no shoes. Left my service and went home to Mr. Home of Bassendean. He was very head-strong and cruel to the Horses which made me tyred of him.

5. John Bashett from the Flas entered in his place. Wages £4 without shoes ye whole year, optional to part at Martinmas.

Wm. Waddle. At this Term I took him as House boy in place of John Henderson who went to Bassendean as his shepherd. Did not keep one in his place, money being scarce and meal dear.

John Basket left after 1 year.

Wm. Waddell − Nota: He has agreed to stay other 2 years. Wages £4 yearly and six sheeps' grass.

To Jas. Jaffray in part . . . £2. 2/− i.e. paid to a/c.

To ditto when his Moyr [Mother] dyed . . . £1. 6. 6d.

The Laird would be exasperated at seeing these young men so unwilling to settle down. The comparison with employees like Rutherfoord, Turnbull, White, Henderson and Neil must have made him very anxious about the future wellbeing of the estate. But he would know from the men who worked for his neighbours and who came to him that the whole of the Borders and beyond were suffering similar unrest. Had they known it, the whole of the Lowlands would soon be searching for farm servants whose wages would be rising inexorably.

As a result of this situation, John Spottiswoode kept looking for reliable craftsmen and from the mid-1770s engaged several who did not stay very long. One of these was Thomas Cossar. The Laird writes: 'He is son to Alex. Cossar, Smith at Westruther and Beedale and Grave digger to the Parish. He was an honest man and had a large family of sons by his first wife and this Thomas by a second. He named one of his sons Walter after the Minister, Walter Scot, the present Minister's father. This Walter was several years from 1737 Schoolmaster of the parish and was, by the influence of Mr. John Gowdie, Minister at Earlestown who married Mr. Walter Scots's eldest daughter − recommended to Mr. Peter Wedderburn, Advocate and afterwards a Lord of Session to go to school with his son and wait upon him. Mr. Wedderburn was then Secretary to the

Board of Excise and got Walter Cossar made a clerk in the Comptroller's office. He then taught writing in Edinburgh and had a very large school and was promoted to be depute Comptroller and now since his pupil, Mr. Alex. Wedderburn was made Solicitor General to the King in England, on the death of the Comptroller, Mr. Penny, he procured the office for Walter Cossar, the salary of which for himself and clerks is odds of £600 sterl., All this surprising good fortune he owes to Mr. Gowdie on account of his being named after his Wife's father.

'In the year 1772 I had a very bad Smith, John Knox, who pric'd [pierced] one of my best horses and high priced and as I had formerely employ'd old Alex. Cossar who was long my Smith and his son having some reputation in his business, I made trial of him'.

Then comes a list of the items a smith would attend to and which Alex Cossar carried out month by month. He also had to make crooks for gates and, of course, supply all the iron and nails himself. The fee he received was half a guinea a horse and calculated every six months. But this did not keep Cossar fully employed. Accordingly, he was asked to make such things as a cover for the boiler which cost the Laird 1s. Then comes a very interesting item: 'By 10 roads [rods] for hanging Window courtings'. This is a clear sign that the lady of the house was no longer willing to rely on shutters for her privacy. She would be having guests, now that the main roads were passable and no longer mere rutted tracks, and this called for fashionable decor. But only for 10 curtain rods! One can hear the Laird protest – only the rooms to be used by guests would have any 'courtings'! Besides, the smith had other items to see to, like making a key to a drawer for 4d. and repairing hub and spokes of a wheel for 6d., as well as shoeing horses.

Why the next entry is put in the Diary under Alex Cossar's account is inexplicable. It is a description of a function where the Parish was divided. It runs as follows: 'By entertainment of meat and drink furnished to the Company at the division of Westruther betwixt Mr Home and you [John Spottiswoode] anno 1772 – £18. 8/– your half £9. 4/–. Nota: Mr. Home caused the Sherif on some pretence clip this account 32 shillings but I paid the above without any deduction for I thought it unreasonable first to take one's meat and drink and then find fault with the price, and the more so when the Bills were given in every meeting and signed without any challenge till they were to be paid'!

Nothing more is said of this occasion and the Laird does not refer to it again. Instead, he reverts to everyday matters, such as having Cossar 'making a new graip' for 6d. and 'mending the chaise axle-tree', also for 6d. At this cost, the damage cannot have been too serious, but still reflects the condition of the roads, especially the cross roads (i.e. side roads). There is then a change. Instead of shoeing horses, as he has done regularly during the past three years, he shoes six oxen which shows how ploughing and other farm work was still done by either oxen or horses. The cost of shoeing oxen was only 6d. each compared with half a guinea for horses. It must be remembered, however, that the fee for horses is on a yearly basis, during which time they might have needed shoeing on several occasions. As to cost, several papers were written at the time giving the comparative costs of using horses or oxen.

A year after mending the chaise, Thomas Cossar had to attend to its wheels, which shows it had taken damage again. But it cannot have been too serious this time, as the charge for the repair was only 6d. Then for the first time, the Diary mentions a farm implement, the grass-barrow for broadcasting grass seed and graithing the new roller, i.e. preparing it for work. The Improvers discovered that a roller could break up clods and give a far better tilth for the sowing of crops than hitherto – especially grass.

At the end of 1778, Thomas Cossar's agreement with the Laird ran out and Andrew Mather took his place. He had once been ploughboy at Spottiswoode and was taken on again because Thomas Cossar 'Was not serving me properly and growing very greedy. I furnish iron and coals while he [Mather] shoes the horses at 3/– a head the whole year. Gets 16/8d for two plows, 5/– for mending hows, hammers or other things and what other work he makes he is to be paid at the common rate of the Country. He began my work this day being Tuesday, 24th June 1777, so the year was to be counted from this day'. Then came the first entry: 'To cash he being to be marry'd . . . £2'.

The division of the Parish of Westruther which John Spottiswoode celebrated with entertainment of food and drink raises at least one important question. Although the Statistical Account, compiled by Sir John Sinclair between 1791 and 1799, mentions this division and gives the name of the Laird of Bassendean, Mr. Home, it does not give John Spottiswoode's name as the other Heritor. It ignores him completely. Why is this?

Is it mere conjecture to suggest that the Laird of Spottiswoode was *persona non grata* with the Kirk authorities and yet what other reason can there be? The family were strongly loyal to the Stuarts and were Episcopalians. Nothing could have estranged them from the established church more than this. Mr. William Shiels, the Minister, may therefore have compiled his report for Westruther in the way he did because he knew it was to be published and there was no point in risking a reprimand, if not worse. Furthermore, Mr. Shiels was in a fairly comfortable situation which he would not wish to forfeit. Who would blame him, because in 1755 the Parish had 501 members; in 1783, 685 members; and in 1791, 730. Either he did not wish to admit the satisfactory growth of the Parish as being mainly due to John Spottiswoode's 50 years of improvements or preferred not to put such a fact on paper for the reason already given. All he said was: 'Upon the application of the Heritors, who complained of the distance of the Church of Gordon, a Minister was appointed in the year 1647 to a chapel at Bassendean'. One year previously, Sir Robert Spottiswoode had been beheaded at St. Andrews and the estate was in the hands of people called Bell. The only heritor with the freedom to act as he wished was the Laird of Bassendean. Mr. William Shiels skipped very adroitly over this problem.

Nevertheless, he admits improvement in the land through manuring, mainly with lime and dung, and he gives an accurate description of the benefits of drying up sodden ground. His list of livestock shows how much the estates of Spottiswoode and Bassendean had been improved. He states that there are now 160 horses in the parish, 700 black cattle and 5,000 sheep and that 'Considerable attention is now paid to the improvement of the breed of stock of every kind'.

Did this include improving the fleece? Mr. Shiels does not comment though he must have seen scores of sheep brought in from the hills in autumn to be smeared with a mixture of tar and butter. He would possibly approve of this supposedly excellent manner of keeping sheep free from maggots and other vermin as well as protecting them against the cold. John Spottiswoode certainly used tar and butter to smear his flock but we do not know for how long he persisted in this. However, from time to time he sells his people 'English wool' which is free from butter and tar and which brought a far higher price. But even this evidence did not seem to persuade either himself or other sheep masters to change their ways. Besides, the nation was girding itself for war and this caused a very firm market for wool which would show a constant rise in value over the next 30 years.

In 1774 the Laird wrote this: 'James Neil, Mason and son to John Neil sometime Miller at the Mill and brother to my servant. When he was a boy I recommended him to Mr. D. Walker Advocat. He served him in Edinburgh several years and when he was grown up he chois'd rather to learn a trade than continue in service. So he left Mr. Walker, came to the country and bound himself 'prentice to a Mason and is a tollerable hewer and builds well. He marry'd a servant of mine, Nell Moffat'.

His first task was to work on the new offices and he agreed to a wage of 14d. per day. It was quite a reasonable wage and probably more than he had with Mr. Walker and certainly more than when he was working as a 'prentice. Being married, he would be offered a cottage and with it the usual payments in kind. But one wonders how he managed to buy a cow of his own – which he did and paid the Laird £4 7s. for it. But the next expense was mandatory – his wife was in labour, so all the usual ritual would have to be gone through, against which he drew 10s. from the Laird. Was this all the Laird would advance or did James Neil restrict himself to 10s.? The chances are the former because Neil owed nearly £13 and had only earned £5.

It was perhaps as well that Neil returned to the work he knew best because that was where he could gain the best wage. But four years after coming to Spottiswoode he was still in debt to the Laird, the amount being £26. What was John Spottiswoode to do? Allow Neil to continue building up debts or give him more lucrative work? John Spottiswoode decided to give him a new farm with a rental of £4 a year. On the face of it, this seems like throwing good money after bad. Be that as it may, Neil was given work which he undertood and where he could earn a better wage – building dykes and then a stable and a barn and a byre. By the end of 1780, he was only owing the Laird £8. Although the Diary does not say so, Neil's wife must have given him considerable help by looking after their little farm, thereby allowing him to spend as much time as possible on dykes and new buildings for which the Laird would pay. There is a typical observation by the Laird. In calculating what Neil owed he recorded this: 'By ye east cross dyke at ye Nursery, north of ye east Avenue at 14d. per rood – 9/11d., ye odd penny cast in for even money'.

But matters had turned worse again for James Neil, his debt to the Laird now standing at about £25 with little sign of improvement. The second last line seems to express the Laird's frustration – '25th. August 1782 – W. Brown and him at ye herring . . . 7/–'. It was hardly work for a qualified mason. However, all trace of James Neil ends there so how he liquidated his debt we do not know. Perhaps he went back to Bassendean Quarry where he had recently worked for 11d. a day.

In 1781 a long-serving man was about to retire. He was an exception in that he was not only a valued craftsman but one of long service and therefore unusual. His name was William Haig, and he was a wright to trade, which meant he could work in either metal or wood. He came to Spottiswoode in 1750 or thereby, the exact date being lost with Ledger C. Working under his father, Alex Haig, he took over in 1766 when the old man died. He had served John Spottiswoode well. The Laird made this final entry: 'I agreed with Wm. Haig as a Servant to take care of the planting work in ye Garden and Wright work or any other work for one year from Whitsun 1781 to Whits 1782 at £6 pound sterling wages, 3 sheeps grass, 6 bolls meal, free house, well looking with proper roofing, but cast and winnowed at his own expense and a cow's grass with winter fodder'.

15

John Spottiswoode's Legacy
to his Successors

How DID the Spottiswoode family regard John who kept the Diary, and what did they do, if anything, to complement his work? John's heir (i.e. John III) was a solicitor in London and therefore we assume took only a spasmodic interest in the estate. He may have kept the books for a while after his father died in 1793, because someone did, but it was, more likely, John II's daughter Rachael. Her name is mentioned several times and she had complete authority to manage the estate. There is no proper Diary/Journal after the death of John II, only some random entries in the closing pages, written by another hand, most probably Rachael's.

At the time of John II's death, agriculture in England was flourishing, on account of her doucer climate. She was enjoying yearly rises in the price of wheat while in Scotland the value of sheep and cattle rose more steadily. The enormous fleet which the country maintained had to be victualled with salt beef and biscuit at every return to port and the armies of the Crown required feeding every day. The Improvers were doing their work well on both sides of the Border, and men were avidly reading the publications which came regularly off the presses to educate farmers and landowners in the latest methods of improved husbandry. They also attended the regular meetings of the Farming Societies which had sprung up on both sides of the Border. Some still exist, one being the West Lothian Discussion Society.

At Spottiswoode, the tenants and the estate itself would see rising profits all through the 20 years of war against Napoleon. There would be money to spend on every kind of improvement, and wherever men gathered at Markets the talk would be of the latest in arable machinery and the state of the year's crops. How did the Spottiswoode Estate respond?

The answer lies in the prosperity of the estate and the capital which was available after John II's death. What his son did and what policies Rachael decided to pursue, is all conjecture. John III would be facing similar problems to those which confronted John Cockburn of Ormiston, because both were domiciled in London and would have run their estates at a distance. But whereas Cockburn left copious notes and letters, John Spottiswoode III left no evidence at all. In any case, he had his sister Rachael at Spottiswoode who saw to the day-to-day management. John III died in 1805, so it was left to his son, John IV, to elect what to do. He too was a man of the law and a J.P. It appears that he appointed a factor, but under Rachael's direction until her death in 1817.

The factor's name was James Black and in the Archives of the Royal Highland and Agricultural Society of Scotland his address is given as Spottiswoode. The paper he submitted to them was entitled 'Account of the Drainage on the Estate of Spottiswoode in the County of Berwick'. It received the Society's Commendation for Excellence and was regarded as a splendid and effective experiment. But in James Black's account, every praise is offered to 'The late Mr. Stephens, who had come to Scotland with a view to the laying out of drains, so little understood in this part of the Kingdom'. But there is another sentence of great import- ance, written by James Black. It is as follows: 'The success of the operation on this property, and some others, and the perfectly simple and satisfactory explanations given by Mr. Stephens induced Mr. Spottiswoode, the Pro- prietor, at once to resolve to act under his guidance'.

The work was begun (according to James Black) in the year 1815 – a significant date to the nation – and was not completed until 1828. In all, 500–600 acres were drained involving 5428 roods, equal to 32,568 yards – or over 18 miles. In some parts, it was found necessary to set the drains down 13 feet, with a medium depth of five to seven feet. And all of this was done by hand. A copy of the drain plan showing each field and the location of each drain has become available, with what looks like Mr. Stephens' proposals and observations superimposed. While James Black was working 'in the field', he also had his eye on the construction of a special piece of tackle for lifting big stones from the surface and those lying hidden below. A drawing of this remarkable implement was shown. However, even this would not lift really big stones from below the surface. These had to be dynamited. The Highland Society again complimented John IV for being the first in Scotland to use this tackle, and then dubbed him 'A most judicious and spirited Improver'. Praise indeed!

It is interesting to read James Black's description of the land as he found it, and to set this information beside what the Diary has revealed about the preparation and digging out of ditches. Had it not been for the low wages and low costs of John II's time, one wonders whether John IV would have tackled the drainage work pronounced by Mr. Stephens as essential. John II was a great worker and exceedingly determined, but to him cost was everything, as his quoted remarks continually show. James Black underlined this point right at the start of his Paper to the Royal Highland: 'Repeated endeavours had been made, at a great expense of money and materials to render these lands dry; but they had either failed entirely or been but partially successful. At the time when the [new] drainage was begun on more correct principles, there was not a field which could be said to be free from wetness'. John IV was thus faced with an enormous problem, both in time and money, and he could easily have walked away and left James Black to do what he could. But what would that determined old warhorse, his grandfather, have said to that?

It appears that the last entry John Spottiswoode II made in the Diary was in July 1785, when he wrote up Andrew Cribbis' account. There is then a gap of five and a half years until the entries begin again in January 1791, written by other hands, only to stop once more until April 1792. The entries of January are reckonings by the estate with men, who were called for the first time 'workmen', and who would have been pressing for what they were due, either because of the old laird's incapacity or because they feared having to wait still longer under a new master. Payment for goods and services resumed and continued throughout 1792.

Looking over these final payments in this addendum to the Diary is most interesting. There was much to do in the garden, apparently. Being April, it was early spring with growth already started, weeds as well as bushes and plants. The gardens and policies of Spottiswoode would give extensive shelter, as they still do, wild and untamed as they now are. Next comes the spring 'Thrishing', when the seed was cleaned and separated by the fanners. This was followed by '11 days at the planting'. In other words the sowing. It would be done by broadcasting by hand from a linen sheet slung round the neck and tied at the waist. The next entry of note is '10 days cleaning grass'. This would be seed saved from the previous season's haymaking which would contain all manner of weed seeds and rubbish. Then comes tragedy: 'To Rob Thorburn 7 days going round the planting blawn by the wind'. Had the old Laird been up and about, this carnage in his new woodlands would have depressed him enormously.

Improvement and planting still continued. There was wood to be laid on the floor of a stable and purchase of garden trees and then clover seed and two spades, together costing over £40. More money for 'the Killn' shows that lime was still being bought (although 'kiln' is at last spelt with an 'n', it still has two 'l's). Roof tiles were now being used for the first time, instead of turf or heather, and there is more lime to be spread. The Loft needed a wooden floor, so 28 trees were felled to supply the necessary timber. These trees must have been quite young, not more perhaps than 30 years. But wood was needed at Spottiswoode, so apart from the 28, a load of seasoned timber was brought by waggon from Leith. The carriage was very reasonable, being only 7s. 6d. A plan was required for Hyndside-hill farm – the only plan which figures in the Diary. Finally, two more carts of young trees were needed and another cart of timber from Leith. It was an expensive month, about £180 being spent.

On page 3 of the addendum the writing changes, to a fine flowing, copperplate style. The mason, Thomas Lockie, and five other men are paid for bringing in stones. Fifty-three carts of lime arrived and for the first time 'sand' is mentioned. This was a mixture of shells and sand, ideal either for spreading on the land or for use in building. But the important entry is the following: 'The sand was driven by our own horses being 150 cart loads equal to 225 hired carts at least'. The Laird had done well in buying that waggon at Kelso! The writing then changes back to the original style.

There was the March dyke to mend between Westruther and Blackhall, but it did not cost much, only 63 roods at a cost of £1 16s. 10d. for the Spottiswoode half.

Hay was the next item. According to the Diary, they cut and turned it in September. The sown grass was the first to be cut and the meadow hay followed, everything being redd up by the end of the month. They were late in doing this as the weather is unreliable in September. But Scots farmers did not bother much about the hay crop until the grain harvest was all led in. But why the delay, when they had taken the trouble to winnow the grass and save the seed? One can hardly see the old Laird ordering things in this way.

On 15th October John Hewat's rent of £60 was received for Flass and Woodheads and immediately paid over to the local minister. This would seem to indicate that the Spottiswoode stipend was in arrears and that the interest received from the bank was being used to liquidate this and other estate debts. For example, payment of Poor's money for Spottiswoode, Wedderlie and Thornydike, outstanding for 1791 and 1792, and also the schoolmaster's salary, were all settled up, making the year 1792 another expensive one. But all landowners had to meet these burdens although none liked doing so. It made schoolmastering a highly hazardous occupation, having to wait for money. The local Kirk Session also had to rely on contributions from the heritors to swell their Poor's fund and often had to wait a considerable time before they received it. This was clearly the case at Spottiswoode. Another burden was the hated land tax. For Spottiswoode it amounted to £33 per year. The minister's stipend for the estate was £16 19s. 5d and for Thornydike £25 12s. 3d.

Many of the old practices still prevailed. For example, it was often the custom to plant a few trees in a tenant's kailyard, in order to shelter his house and later to provide him with a small supply of timber. In February of 1793, which was just a month before the Laird died, some trees were planted in George and James Grahames' kailyard. The Diary notes the various kinds, namely, 'Silver fir sprus [sic], Birch of which kinds 20 a peace were planted'. A month after the funeral, William Hog's yard had planted in it '20 Silver fir, 10 sprus, 6 Birch, 2 Oaks, 2 Plaines' while Andrew Shiel of Dods got '20 silver fir planted'.

The total money spent since the bank interest arrived had now reached the very large sum for those days of £541 8s. 11d. (and ten twelfths of a penny!).

By the time page 4 of the addendum is reached, there is a much more moderate rate of spending, which surely means that the estate debts had been largely paid off. Nevertheless, there are several intriguing entries. A farm servant by the unusual name of Basta Henderson spent three days mending 'the dike Tollbar'. This is the first time mention is made of any Spottiswoode Toll Bar. One wonders what damaged it. Was some vehicle responsible? The only information we can glean is that it took three days to mend at 1s. a day.

More trees arrived from Edinburgh, which may have been bought to replace those 'blawn by the wind'. The rent for Scott's House in the Canongate of Edinburgh was paid, but this time it amounted to £5, an increase of £2 on the previous payment.

The sum of 13s. 9d. was spent on killing 100 moles. Such a large number would almost certainly make the garden look unkempt.

A further £22 was spent on buying trees – and then a strange item: 'To cleaning and taking down the Houses at Thimble[hall] and cleaning the Hedge and dikers leading stones for £9 10 6d.'. It looks as though the old, badly built houses with their rubble walls and turf or heather roofs were being taken down and replaced with stone-built houses with proper roof tiles. All these expenses came to £44 1s. 3d.

Page 5 is a very interesting page. It begins with an explanation of a Teviotdale Boll which consists of three half-firlots of oats. A Boll of Oats was 6 bushels – on average 252lbs. A firlot was one quarter of this, or 63lbs, a half firlot therefore being 31lbs. 'It was all sowen in the Rouan tree park'.

The next purchase covered four bolls of rye grass seed. This was for sowing and May month was considered the best time for doing so. A boll probably weighed about 140lbs and the sowing rate (by hand) would be around 36/40lbs per acre.

Then came a record of payment for 15 months of Donaldson's News-paper, costing £1 17s. 6d. It is not a large amount but the fact that it was not paid for fully 15 months is another possible indication that money had been scarce or that the Laird had been too ill to attend to it. There was no newspaper of that name circulating at the time, but there was a business in Edinburgh called James Donaldson which handled *The Edinburgh Ad-vertiser*. It would therefore seem that Donaldson delivered news-sheets to the Spottiswoode house in the Canongate and had been calling for his money.

A domestic matter is recorded with the terse entry: 'To a hat to James . . . 2/6d'. James was not a member of the family, and as no reason is given why he should have qualified for a new hat, we have to surmise. A James Brown figured in the following month (June 1793), being given £9 3s. 'To pay some ditchers'. Was he a grieve or factor? Or was he a Brown of Thornydike? Whoever he was, he also merited being given 'a pair of breeches' a month later, costing 10s. 1d.

A man called John Bell figures in June of the same year and also a James Bell (who had a smallholding for which he paid a rent of £5 per annum). Were they perhaps relatives of the Bell family who held the estate from the death of Sir Robert Spottiswoode in 1646 (the year of his execution for treason) until 1700 when it was bought back from them by John Spottiswoode I? But Bell was a common Border name.

The page ends with one cart having led out dung for three days at 3s. a day and 'two Wiman filling [i.e. the dung cart] for 3 days a peace [sic]'. This had been the practice for generations in the north, where a wife was prized much higher than a horse. A wife could carry her dung creel on her back while she held the distaff in her free hand!

The last page of all is written in two different styles and concerns mundane matters such as the purchase of nails for the horse and cow-park gates and for putting up the paling at Thornydike. But it also deals with important financial matters. Mrs. Roberton's name is mentioned several times. Judging from the loose note regarding transactions with her, she was certainly in a position of trust as well as being owed over £800 – a very considerable sum in those days. We know she was a member of the family and one who knew about the day-to-day management of the estate. But why did she cease writing up the Diary/Journal almost as soon as the old man died?

Another question arises. One hundred and eighty pounds were drawn 'from Mansfield'. Was he a man or a firm of solicitors or bankers? From evidence available, James and John Mansfield were merchants in Edinburgh as well as directors of the Royal Bank of Scotland (1744 to 1751 and 1760 to 1761). It was quite common at that time for money loans to be made by city merchants to landowners like John Spottiswoode. They would even borrow large sums from the banks in order to lend out small sums to farmers, especially Improvers, at a higher rate than the banks would ask. This naturally pleased the banks as lending costs were minimised and the 'borrowing market' was there and available should the banks ever want it. In due course they did as borrowing levels kept rising (see Neil Munro: *History of The Royal Bank of Scotland*).

Towards the end of the final page is an entry which is much less important by comparison. The mysterious James is given £1 'to py Mr. Stobo'. After that there are the various transactions with Mrs. Roberton followed by a clear indication of how the standard of social life was rising – 'To weaving 24 napkins paid Ebenezer Gardner £1.0.0'.

The old lion, John Spottiswoode, died on March 12th 1793. After that there is no proper Diary, only some random entries in the closing pages, most probably in the hand of his daughter Rachael. A touching entry informs us that two dozen bottles of port were taken out of the cellar for his funeral. Port had figured in the Diary since August 1789, when John laid down 48 dozen, perhaps in anticipation of the sources of supply drying up. He was probably, like many of his contemporaries, a regular buyer of smuggled wine and spirits. It is recorded that the entire seacoast from Berwick to Prestonpans was occupied by one connected line of smugglers all acquainted with each other (*Statistical Account*, 1835). At any rate consumption in the house rose steadily, until it fell away after his death.

The increased consumption of port may have been due in part to the greater activity and socialising arising from more money in circulation and better transport. While money was tight, as we know, the state of the roads prevented trade from expanding between town and town and city and city. Even trading between individuals was affected. Agricultural leases were often too short, and rack-renting was the constant fear of the tenant. We do not know how they fared at Spottiswoode, only how the estate was managed and how the Laird doggedly tried to improve it. But communications were hindered at every turn, and improving them seemed quite beyond either Government or individual. An example of this was shown in the surprise of the people at seeing in 1723 a small load of coal being brought by cart from Kilbride to Cambuslang when 'crowds of people went out to see the wonderful machine'. It was made of solid wooden wheels, revolving with the wooden axle-trees. They did not come into common use in the Lowlands until 1760. Henry Grey Graham states that in Nairnshire, carts were wholly made of birch, without any iron, costing 6s. 8d. (*Social Life in Scotland in the Eighteenth Century*).

The Government did what it could to improve communications. By statute, able-bodied men in every district were required to give six days' labour in improving the highways, now called Statute Labour Roads. But like so many other measures, this one was also quietly ignored. The dreadful roads caused judges to 'ride on circuit' instead of trying to travel by chaise.

But if individuals, even judges, could ride as they always had done, improved transport was much more necessary for the carriage of bulk materials, and just about the most important of these to an improver like John Spottiswoode was lime. Lime figures largely in the Diary from 1765 onwards, and is closely associated with problems of transport and tolls. Although no mention is made of exactly where his supplies of lime came from, there were several places in the Merse and the Lothians where kilns had been built, the ruins of which can still be seen today. In the Spottiswoode account of lime purchases and transport, it is obvious that distance was all-important. Indeed, it can be seen that in many cases the cost of transport was higher than the price of the lime. We can therefore assume that the east coast would most likely be the main source of 'shells', with the south bank of the Forth estuary and the Lothian coal mines a possibility for other grades of lime. But the lime quarries at Creightoundean, between Pathhead and Faladam, were nearest, and these would surely be the ones operated by 'one Clapperton'.

Lime as a fertiliser and conditioner of wet or acid lands had been known long before John Spottiswoode experimented with it in the mid-eighteenth century. With hindsight, we know that his land was indeed wet and in parts very wet. It was therefore bound to benefit from a dressing of lime, as his *Nota* confirms. Nevertheless, to have spent over £40 on it was a great sum of money in those days, even when spread over three years. There are other points of interest arising from his Account of Lime. There is some detail of a turnpike road from Deanburn Bridge at the foot of Soutra hill near Fala. Either it was never built or was removed, because there is nothing in the Thomson Atlas of 1822 to indicate where it was. There is no indication in Taylor & Skinner either (1776). However, the Laird confirms that his supplies of 'powdered lime were carried on horses' backs'. How much? Three Lothian bolls each, the Laird says, which was something in the order of two hundredweight. They cost 10d. per boll, i.e. 2s. 6d. per cart, with carriage amounting to 5s. each cart. But this was too high, as the Laird indicates, and he managed to agree with James Brockie in Fala at 6d. per horse less. This arrangement shows yet again how tight was the money supply and how hard one had to bargain. The Laird proves the point when he beats Brockie down and makes him agree to deliver one cart free for every 20 he brought to Spottiswoode and to agree also to a discount of '3/9d for ready money'. Dung was also becoming very much sought after at this time, a fact that the Laird would not overlook. On his trips to Edinburgh he would be bound to see scores of carts collecting dung from the city streets and taking it to the farms a few miles away.

The men at Spottiswoode would quickly see the benefit of lime in improved crops and yields. John II certainly did and we have cast-iron proof of this. In 1779 he calculated how his grain yields had turned out, in much the same way as a farmer would do today. His yield for the times was good and probably better than average for the district. The figures show a yield of about 5 to 1, but it was possibly somewhat higher as the stacks lay untouched for about eight months, allowing vermin to rob them and even some thieving by humans and hens. It can therefore be safely assumed that the net yield would be about 6 or 7 to 1. In many parts of Scotland at that time, a normal yield often varied between 3 to 1 and 4 to 1, but sometimes as low as 2 to 1. It is interesting to note that the work and chaise horses were fed generously from the grain yield. Compare that with the evidence of the Statistical Account for Haddington-shire (East Lothian) as late as 1835, which states: 'it was a common employment for the farm servants in the summer afternoons to gather thistles from among the corn or wherever else they could be found, to feed their work-horses during the night, thistles being the only green food the animals ever tasted'.

A sceptic might remark that feeding thistles to work horses hardly indicated progress or even sensible upgrading of hitherto untamed and unfenced land. But improvements came gradually, often stimulated by word of mouth and through Discussion Societies, not to forget careful and cautious experiment by the landowner himself. One must not forget the 'battle of the trees', when arboriculture was literally hated by country people who saw it only as installing shelter and feed for birds. These people lived very close to starvation, especially in the higher and wetter districts, and regarded any departure from the ancient ways of the 'farm touns' as the Devil's work.

Family tradition has it that the Spottiswoodes regarded themselves as farmers first and foremost. If so, that interest of theirs must be seen alongside their attachment to the law. But it must have been the case with John Spottiswoode II. He would not tolerate either poor workmanship or slackness and said so in the Diary. There is proof also of a family urge to impress in the detail given about the Spottiswoode Ox. Here is a cattle-beast, of enormous height and girth, weighing close on a ton and a half. If ever proof was needed of the Spottiswoode land being good enough to raise well-bred cattle of record-breaking size, here was that unchallengeable proof. Furthermore, other farmers seeing this incredible animal would know there were others behind it in the Spottiswoode herd. Men would say that cattle bought from that estate were bound to be 'cracking beasties' of great potential, and up would go the price! The Spottiswoode reputation would rise with it.

There are other indications of the Estate being among the most go-ahead in Berwickshire, such as the enormous drainage programme instigated by John IV and the continuous forestry plantings and harvesting. There was also the lavish use of lime which John II indulged in and the elaborate arrangements for its transportation, at a time when carts were wooden sledges.

John IV was a mighty man in his ancestral country, much solicited for his advice and his name. Certainly in its last years, and probably in his time too, the Estate provided some of the finest shooting in the Borders; bags of a thousand and more were commonplace.

For all this, the foundation was laid by John II with the careful, laborious work chronicled in the Diary. Undoubtedly, he fully deserves inclusion in the distinguished list of Berwickshire Improvers.

Index